Mrs. Lee's Stories About
God's First People
Mrs. Irven Lee

Illustrated by
Celia Swafford and Mrs. Bennie Lee Fudge

ISBN 10: 1-58427-391-7

ISBN 13: 978-158427-391-2

Guardian of Truth Foundation
CEI Bookstore
220 S. Marion St., Athens, AL 35611
1-855-49-BOOKS or 1-855-492-6657
www.CEIbooks.com

TO OUR GRANDCHILDREN:
KIRK, KEVAN, LAURA, AND RYAN

God Made the World

(Gen. 1:1-31)

The Bible is the best book in the world. It tells about God and Jesus. God and Jesus live up in Heaven. The Holy Spirit and the angels live in Heaven with God and Jesus.

The Bible tells us that God made the world. Jesus helped him make the world. When God first made the world, it was not pretty, the way it is now. Everything was dark, and nothing could grow on it. God said, "Let there be light, and there was light." He made the sky and the clouds. He made the water run into the rivers and the ocean so the ground could be dry. When the

5

ground was nice and dry, he made plants on the earth. Plants are things like trees and flowers and vegetables.

God made the sun to shine in the day to make the earth warm and light. He made the moon and stars to shine at night. He made birds to fly in the sky, and he made fish to swim in the water. He made animals to walk on the ground. Animals are like dogs and cats and horses and cows.

Last of all, God made a man to live on the earth. He called the man Adam. He told Adam to take care of all the things that he had made.

When God looked at everything that he had made, he saw that it was very good. He rested then from all his work. He did not rest because he was tired because God never gets tired, but he rested because he had finished everything he wanted to do. He had made a beautiful world, and he had made a man to live in the beautiful world. He brought all the animals to the man for him to see. Adam looked at all the animals and gave names to all of them.

QUESTIONS

1. What is the best book in the world?
2. About whom does the Bible tell us?
3. Where do God and Jesus live?
4. Who else lives in Heaven?
5. Who made the world?
6. How did the earth look at first?
7. What did God say?
8. Name some of the things that God made.
9. What did God make last of all?
10. What did God call the man?
11. What did God do when he had finished his work?
12. What did Adam do when he saw all the animals?

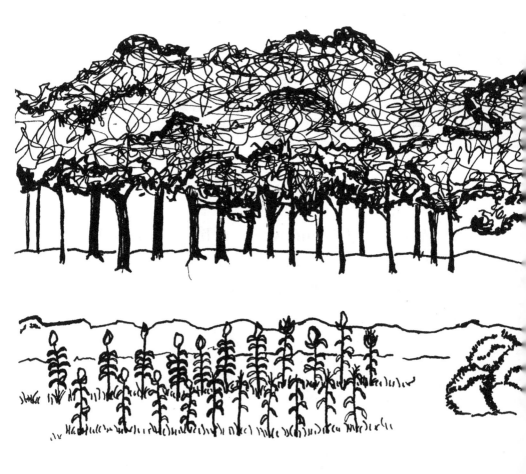

The Garden and the Woman
(Gen. 2:8-25)

God planted a beautiful garden in Eden so the man could have a pretty place to live. We call it the Garden of Eden. It was not a little garden like the kind we have where we grow vegetables. It was a big, big garden, so big that there were four rivers around it. It had many trees in it. It had every-thing growing in it that was pretty and everything that was good to eat. God told Adam to take care of all the trees and keep them just as pretty as they were when God made them.

The fruit on the trees was good, and it was pretty. God told Adam that he could eat of all the fruit in the garden except the fruit of the tree that grew in the middle of the garden. The tree in the middle of the garden was different

from all the other trees. God said that Adam must not eat of it because if he did, he would die.

The man was living all alone in the pretty garden. The animals were there, but they could not talk to him. God saw that the man was alone. He said, "It is not good that the man should be alone." He said he would make some one to be with him.

God made Adam go to sleep. While he was asleep, God opened his side and took out a rib. He made a woman out of the rib. When Adam waked up from his sleep, God brought the woman to him. Adam called her name Eve. He said she was part of him because she was made from his rib.

The man and the woman lived together in the beautiful garden and took care of it. They were good and

they were happy. God walked in the garden and talked with them just as we talk with one another.

QUESTIONS

1. What did God plant?
2. What do we call the garden?
3. Was it a little garden like our gardens?
4. What was in the garden?
5. Whom did God put to live in the garden?
6. Of how many of the trees could the man eat?
7. Of how many could he not eat?
8. Where was the one he could not eat?
9. What did God say would happen if the man did eat of that tree?
10. What did God say when he saw that the man was alone?
11. Tell how God made the woman.
12. What did Adam call her?
13. What kind of work did the man and woman do?
14. Who walked and talked with them in the garden?

The Sin of Adam and Eve
(Gen. 3:1-24)

Satan is the bad man. We call him the devil. He tries to get people to do wrong so that God will punish them. He does not want people to do good things. He can change himself to look like other things so that we will not know who he is.

Adam and Eve were living in the beautiful garden of Eden. They were very happy because they were doing the things that God told them to do. People are always happy when they are doing what God tells them to do.

Satan did not want Adam and Eve to be happy. He did not want them to do what God told them to do. He changed himself into a serpent so they would not know who he was. A serpent is a big snake. The serpent came to Eve and began to talk to her. He asked her if God had said she could eat the fruit of all the trees in the garden. Eve told him that God said they could eat of every tree except one. They must not eat of the tree in the middle of the garden. She said they must not even touch that tree. God had said if they ate of it, they would die. Satan said, "You will not die." He said if she ate of it she would become very wise and would know many things. She would know good things and bad things. Now, Eve already knew good things, and she did not need to know bad things.

Eve looked at the tree. She saw that the fruit was pretty, and it looked good to eat. She wanted to be very wise, and she wanted to know good things and bad things. She took some of the fruit and ate it. She gave some to Adam, and he ate it also.

After they had eaten the fruit, they heard the voice of God walking in the garden. He called to them and said, "Where are you?" They were hiding. God asked them why they were hiding. Adam said, "I heard your voice in the garden, and I was afraid." God knew that they had done wrong. He said, "Have you eaten of the tree that I commanded you not to eat?"

Adam said, "The woman whom thou gavest to be with me, she gave me of the tree, and I did eat."

God said to the woman, "What have you done?" She said that the serpent had played a trick on her and had told her a story. She had believed what he said, and she ate of the fruit.

They had disobeyed God. They had done what he told them not to do. Since they had done wrong, God said they could not live in the pretty garden any more. He drove them out of the garden, and he put an angel at the gate to keep them from going back into it. He told them that they would have to work hard now. Weeds and thorns would grow in their way and make their work harder. He said that after a while they would die, and everybody who would live in the world after them would have to die also.

God punished the serpent. He made him crawl on the ground. He could not walk and talk any more. God said that he would make all people hate the snake.

QUESTIONS

1. Who is Satan?
2. What does he want people to do?
3. Why were Adam and Eve happy in the garden?
4. What did Satan look like when he came to Eve?
5. What did he ask her?
6. What did she tell him?
7. Why could they not eat of that tree?
8. What did Satan say would happen if they ate of the tree?
9. Why did Eve eat the fruit?
10. Who else ate the fruit?
11. What did God say that the man and the woman would have to do?
12. How did he keep them from going back into the garden?
13. What did he say would grow to make their work harder?
14. How did God punish the serpent?

Cain and Abel
(Gen. 4:1-15)

Adam and Eve had a little baby boy. He was the first little baby ever to be born in the world. They named him Cain. After that they had another little boy, and they named him Abel.

The boys grew up and became men. Abel became a shepherd, and Cain became a farmer. That means that Abel raised sheep and Cain raised things in the field.

In those days people did not worship God the way we do now. They did not go to church and sing and pray. God wanted them to do things in a different way. He told them to kill a cow or a sheep or a goat and burn it on an altar. The altar was a pile of big rocks put together to look a little like a table. The people could put the cow or sheep or goat on top and put a fire under it and burn the animal. That was called offering a sacrifice. When the animal was burning, the smoke would go up to the sky. God could smell the smoke, and he would know that the people loved him and were worshipping him.

Abel loved God and wanted to do everything he said. He took a nice fat sheep that was just the kind that God liked and offered a sacrifice. God smelled the smoke and he knew that Abel loved him. He was pleased with Abel.

Cain did not love God. He did not care if he did the wrong thing. He took some of the things he raised in the field and offered a sacrifice. God smelled the smoke from the altar, and it did not smell right. He knew that Cain did not love him. He was not pleased with him.

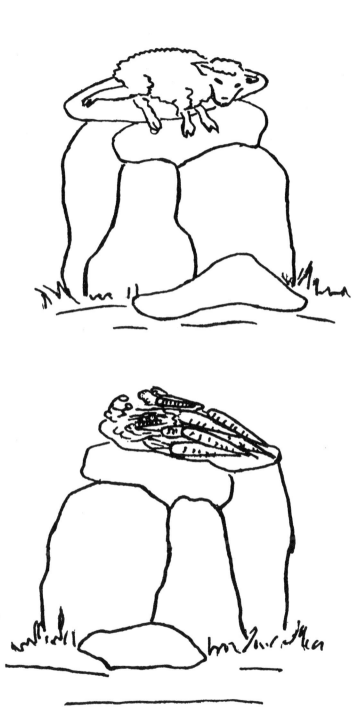

He told Cain that he had done wrong and that Abel had done right.

It made Cain very angry with Abel because he had done wrong and Abel had done right. He was so angry with him that when they were out in the field together where nobody could see them, he killed him.

After a while God called Cain and said, "Where is Abel, your brother?" Cain said, "I know not. Am I my brother's keeper?" That means, "I don't know. Do I have to take care of my brother?" God told him that he had told a story because Abel's blood was crying to God. God knew what Cain had done, and he did not like it. It is very, very bad to kill some one.

God told Cain that he was going to punish him because he had killed his brother. He told him he would have to leave his home and go away where he would not have a home any more. Cain had been raising things in the field. God said that the ground would not grow good things for him any more. Cain said that God had made his punishment very bad.

QUESTIONS

1. Who was the first baby born in the world?
2. Who was his brother?
3. What kind of work did Cain and Abel do?
4. How did God tell the people then to worship him?
5. How did Abel worship God?
6. How did Cain worship God?
7. Which one pleased God?
8. Why was Cain angry with Abel?
9. What did he do when nobody was looking?
10. What did God ask Cain?
11. What did Cain say?
12. How did God punish Cain?

God's Heart Becomes Sad

(Gen. 6:1-13)

Adam and Eve had another boy, and they named him Seth. Eve said that God gave him to them because Cain had killed Abel. Seth looked like his father. After that, Adam and Eve had more children, but we do not know their names. Soon there were many, many people living on the earth.

When there were lots of people on the earth, some of them loved God and some of them did not love him. A great number of the people began to do things that God did not like. He said that the people were doing bad things and they were even thinking bad thoughts.

It made God's heart very sad because the people were doing bad things. He said he was sorry that he had ever made any people to live on the earth. He said, "I will destroy all the people on the earth because I am sorry I ever made them." Destroy means to kill or to get rid of. He said he was so sorry that he was going to destroy all the animals and all the birds, too.

There was one man on the earth who did not do bad things and did not think bad thoughts. His name was Noah. He was good, and he was sorry that all the other people were bad. He loved God and did the things that God told him to do.

Noah had a wife and he had three sons. His sons' names were Shem, Ham, and Japheth. The sons had wives, too. Noah's wife and his sons and his sons' wives were all good. God loved all of them.

One day God told Noah that he was

sad because all the people were bad and he wished he had not made them. He told Noah that he was going to destroy the people and the birds and all the animals. He said that he would not destroy Noah and his family because they were good.

In our next story I will tell you how God destroyed all the bad people and how he saved Noah and his family.

QUESTIONS

1. Name another son of Adam and Eve.
2. Why did Eve say God gave him to them?
3. Did Adam and Eve have any more children?
4. What did many people begin to do?
5. Why was God's heart sad?
6. What did he wish?
7. What did he say he was going to do?
8. What does "destroy" mean?
9. Can you name one good man?
10. Can you name his three sons?
11. What did God tell Noah?
12. Was God going to destroy Noah and his family? Why not?

The Ark and the Flood
(Gen. 6:14 - 8:5)

God told Noah that the people on the earth were bad and that he was going to destroy them. Noah and his family were good, so God was going to save them.

God told Noah to build an ark. An ark is a boat house. This ark was to be real long, real wide, and real high. It was to be bigger than any of our houses. It was to have three stories in it. That means there was to be a downstairs and an upstairs and another upstairs. There was to be just one window, and it was to be in the very top so nobody could see out. There was to be one door in the side of the ark.

Noah did everything just as God told him, and he built the ark. He made the top and the sides and the bottom so they would not let any water come into

the ark.

God told Noah to get some of every kind of food that can be eaten and put it in the ark. He told him to get some of every kind of animals and birds and put them in the ark. Noah did all that God told him, and he did it just the way God said.

Noah made the ark and it was finished. He put in all the food and the animals and the birds. Then God told him to bring all his family. Noah did just as God said, and he and all his family went into the ark. God shut the door and shut them inside.

In seven days it began to rain. It was the biggest rain in all the world. We call it the flood. It rained for forty days and forty nights. It did not stop raining in all that time. It rained so much that all the rivers and the lakes ran over on the land. It rained until all the houses and all the trees were covered with water. It rained until all the mountains were covered.

The bad people on the earth who did not love God could not find a dry place to stay, so they were killed by all the water.

Noah and his family were safe in the ark because they had obeyed God. The ark floated on the top of the water just like a boat. It kept floating until the rain stopped and the water went down off the ground.

When the water went down off the tops of the mountains, the ark stopped and rested on one of the mountains. The name of the mountain was Ararat. Noah could not go out of the ark yet because the water was still on all the low ground. He had to wait until all the water was gone and God opened the door of the ark.

QUESTIONS

1. What did God tell Noah to build?
2. What is an ark?
3. How many stories did the ark have?
4. How many doors did it have?
5. How many windows did it have?
6. What was Noah to put in the ark?
7. When the ark was ready, what did God tell Noah to do?
8. Who shut Noah and his family in?
9. What happened when Noah and his family had been in the ark seven days?
10. How long did it rain?
11. What happened to all the bad people?
12. Were Noah and his family killed? Why not?
13. What did the ark do when the water went off the mountains?
14. Why could Noah not leave the ark yet?

The Flood Is Over
(Gen. 8:6 - 9:17)

God did not forget Noah and his
family. He knew that they were still
shut up in the ark. They stayed in the
ark a little over a year. God made a
wind blow over the land to take the
water away.

Noah thought maybe the water was
gone from the ground. He opened the
window and let a raven fly out. A raven
is a big, shiny, black bird. The raven
could fly around a long time and find
food to eat, so it did not come back to
the ark.

Noah waited a while and he sent out a
dove. A dove is a small, gray bird. It
likes to eat green leaves. The water was
still on the ground, and the dove could
not find anything to eat. It came back
to the ark. Noah opened the window

and let it in.

Noah waited seven days and sent the dove out again. This time it stayed until the evening and it came back to the ark. It had a green leaf in its mouth. Noah knew that the water had gone down from the trees. He waited seven more days and sent the dove out again for the third time. This time it did not come back. Noah knew then that the water was all gone from the earth. He took the top off the ark and looked out. The ground was dry and everything was fresh and new.

God spoke to Noah and told him to go out of the ark and take all his family out. He told him to take all the animals and birds out, too. Noah did just as God told him, and all came out of the ark.

Noah took an animal and offered a

sacrifice to God. He loved God and he was thanking him for taking care of him and his family in the flood. When God smelled the smoke from the altar, he was pleased. He said he would never bring another flood on the earth to destroy all the people. He told Noah that he would put the rainbow in the sky so that every time people look at it they can know that God will never bring another flood on the earth.

QUESTIONS

1. How long did Noah and his family stay in the ark?
2. How did God take the water away?
3. What kind of bird did Noah send out of the ark first?
4. What kind of bird did he send out next?
5. Why did the dove come back?
6. What did the dove bring back in its mouth the second time?
7. How long did Noah wait before sending the dove out again?
8. When the dove did not come back the third time, what did Noah know?
9. What did God tell Noah to do?
10. What was the first thing Noah did when he left the ark?
11. What did God say when he smelled the smoke from the altar?
12. What did God put in the sky to show that he would not bring another flood?

The Tower of Babel
(Gen. 11:1-9)

When the flood was over, Noah and his family were the only people in the world. Before long Noah's sons had children. Soon their children grew to be men and women, and they had children also. After a while there were many people in the world again.

The people wanted to stay together and all live in one place. They did not want to be scattered from each other. They said, "Let us build a city, and let us build a tower in the city that will be so high it will reach all the way to heaven." If the tower reached all the way to the sky, the people could see it a long way and they would not get lost from one another.

They made bricks and got everything ready and began to build the city and the tower. Just when they had the work started and it was not yet finished, God came down to see what they were doing. He knew they wanted to build a tower that would reach all the way to heaven. He was not pleased with them. He said he must stop them because if he did not they would keep on doing things he did not want them to do.

All the people talked just the same way and they could all understand each other. God said if they could not understand each other they would have to stop their work. He mixed up their speech and made them so that they talked differently. They could not understand each other, so they could not work together.

When they could not work together, the people did not want to live together any more. They began to leave their homes and go to other places to live. That was just what God wanted them to do. He wanted people to live in all the countries and not all in one place.

The city and the tower were left not finished. The people called the name of the city Babel.

QUESTIONS

1. Who were the only people on the earth after the flood?
2. How did there get to be more people?
3. What did the people want to do?
4. What did they say to each other?
5. What did they make to use to build the city?
6. Who came down to see what they were doing?
7. What did he say he must do? Why?
8. How did the people talk then?
9. Why did God mix up their speech?
10. What did they do when they could not understand each other?
11. Where did God want people to live?
12. What did they name the city?

The Call of Abraham
(Gen. 11:27 - 12:9)

There was a man named Abraham who lived in the city of Ur. He was a good man and he loved God. His father's name was Terah and his wife's name was Sarah. He had a brother named Haran, and Haran had a son named Lot. Haran died, so his brother Abraham had to take care of Lot. Abraham was Lot's uncle.

One day God talked to Abraham. He told him to leave his father's house and all his kinsfolk and his country and go into a new land. The people around Abraham were bad. They worshipped idols. That means they made things out of gold or silver or wood and worshipped them. God did not like that at all. He wanted Abraham to go into a new land where he could worship God in

45

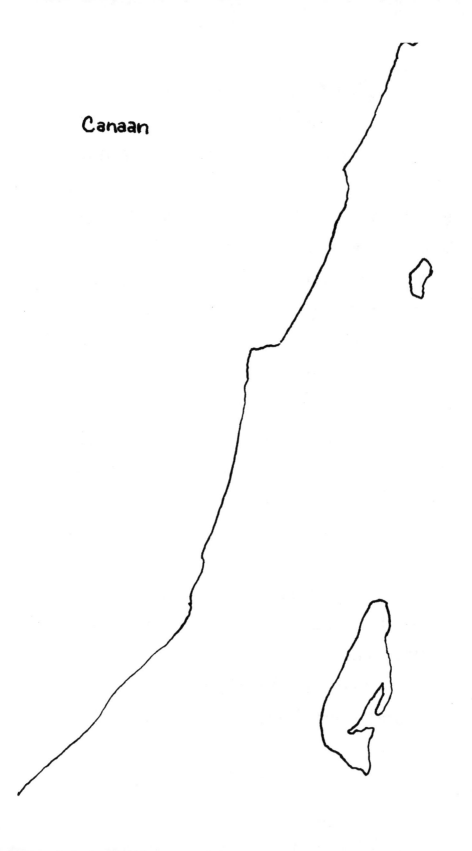

Canaan

the right way.

Abraham did not know where the new land was, but he believed that God would take care of him and show him the way. He obeyed God and did just what he said.

He took his wife Sarah and his father Terah and his nephew Lot and started to the new country. They went for a while until they came to a city called Haran. The city had the same name as Abraham's brother who had died.

Abraham, Sarah, Terah, and Lot stopped and lived in the city of Haran for a while. Terah was real old and the time came for him to die. He died there in the city of Haran.

After Terah was dead, God told Abraham to leave Haran and go on into the new country that he would show him. Abraham took Sarah and Lot and

started. God showed him the way to go. They came to a country called Canaan. That was the place God wanted them to live. It was a good country.

Abraham and Lot raised sheep. They needed lots of green grass for the sheep to eat and lots of fresh water for the sheep to drink. There was plenty of green grass and fresh water in the land of Canaan. Abraham and Lot could be happy there.

Abraham did not live in a house the way we do. He lived in a tent. He could take his tent down and carry it with him. In that way he could move often. He could take his sheep to new places in the land where there was new grass and better water. He moved from place to place, but he lived all the time in the new country of Canaan that God showed to him.

QUESTIONS

1. Where did Abraham live?
2. What kind of man was he?
3. What was his father's name?
4. What was his wife's name?
5. What happened to his brother Haran?
6. What was Haran's son's name?
7. Who had to take care of Lot?
8. What did God tell Abraham to do?
9. Who showed him the way to go?
10. Who died in the city of Haran?
11. When Terah was dead, what did God tell Abraham to do?
12. What was the name of the new country that God showed Abraham?
13. What kind of work did Abraham and Lot do?
14. Why did Abraham move from place to place?

Abraham in Egypt

(Gen. 12:10-20)

One time there came a famine in the land of Canaan where Abraham lived. A famine was a time when no grass could grow for the sheep, and the water was not good for them to drink. Usually a famine came when it had not rained in a long time. Abraham did not have grass for his sheep to eat and he did not have food for himself and his family. They were all hungry.

There was a country not very far away called Egypt. The famine was not in Egypt, so the people there had plenty to eat. Abraham decided to take his wife and go down into Egypt and live there until the famine was over in the land of Canaan.

When they started to Egypt, Abraham was worried about something. He said that Sarah was very pretty. She was much prettier than the women who lived in Egypt. He said he was afraid the people would kill him so they could have the pretty woman. He told her to tell everybody that she was his sister instead of his wife. Then they would not kill him. It is wrong to tell things that are not true, so Abraham and Sarah did wrong.

When they came to Egypt, the people saw them and they saw that Sarah was very pretty. She told them that she was Abraham's sister and that he was her brother. One of the men told the king about her. The king wanted to see her. He took her to his house and wanted to marry her. He treated Abraham very kindly because he thought he was Sarah's brother.

God looked down and saw what

Abraham and Sarah had done. He was not pleased. He is never pleased when people do wrong. He punished the king and all the people because the king had Sarah in his house. The king called Abraham and scolded him for telling that Sarah was his sister. He told him to take Sarah and all that he had and leave the land of Egypt.

Abraham took his wife and went back to the land of Canaan. The famine was over, and there was plenty of grass and water again in the land.

QUESTIONS

1. Why were Abraham and his family hungry?
2. Where did they decide to go?
3. Why was Abraham worried when they started?
4. What did he tell Sarah to do?
5. Is it right to tell things that are not true?
6. When the people of Egypt saw Sarah, what did they think?
7. What did she tell them?
8. Who heard about her?
9. What did the king do?
10. What did God do when he saw what Abraham and Sarah had done?
11. What did the king tell Abraham to do?
12. Where did Abraham and Sarah go to live?

Abraham and Lot
(Gen. 13:1-18)

Abraham was very rich. He had gold and silver. He had cows and sheep. He had lots of servants. Lot lived with him and he was rich, too.

Abraham and Lot had so many sheep and so many cows that there was not enough grass and water for all of them. The place was not big enough for all of them to live together.

One day the servants who took care of Abraham's sheep and the servants who took care of Lot's sheep began to fuss and to scold one another. Each one wanted the best grass and the freshest water. Abraham saw them scolding each other. He went to Lot and told him that it was not right to have trouble. He said they were in the same family. They were kin to each other. He did

not want them to scold and fuss over grass and water. He told Lot that the land was big and there was plenty of room for all of them. He said that Lot could pick out any part of the land that he wanted and go to live in it. Abraham would take the part that was left.

Abraham was old and he had always taken care of Lot. He ought to have had the very best, but Lot was selfish and wanted the best for himself. Lot looked around and saw on one side mountains and hills. He saw on the other side the river of Jordan. He knew that grass would grow better around the river and it would be a better place for the sheep. He picked out the part by the river and took his sheep and servants there. He thought he was taking the very best, but there was a very, very bad city called Sodom close to the river. Lot

would have to live near the bad city.

Abraham took the mountains and the rough part of the country, but he had the best after all. It was not the best place for sheep, but it was a better place to live. There was not a bad city near, and God was with Abraham. When

God is with you, it does not matter if the land is not good. We can always have a good place to live if God is living with us.

QUESTIONS

1. What did Abraham have to make him rich?
2. Who lived with Abraham?
3. What did the servants of Abraham and the servants of Lot begin to do?
4. Why were they fussing?
5. Why did Abraham say they should not quarrel and fuss?
6. What did he tell Lot to do?
7. Which one should have had the best?
8. What did Lot see when he looked around?
9. Which part did he pick out?
10. What was the name of the bad city near the river?
11. Which part did Abraham take?
12. Which one got the best after all? Why?

Hagar and Ishmael
(Gen. 16:1-16)

Abraham was getting old and his wife Sarah was old, too. They were rich. They had lots of gold and silver and servants and sheep, but they did not have any children. God told them that he would give them a son, but they waited and waited and still they did not have a little child. I guess they got tired of waiting, so they began to think of something they could do.

Sarah had a servant whose name was Hagar. She told Abraham that she would give Hagar to him to be his wife. In those days men often had more than one wife, but it was not good. Sarah said that maybe Abraham and Hagar could have a little boy. She said she would call the little boy hers because Hagar was her servant.

Abraham took Hagar to be his wife, and they were going to have a little baby boy. When Hagar knew that she was going to get the little baby boy, she began to think that she was better than Sarah because Sarah did not have any little children. She did not like Sarah any more and would not mind her. Servants are supposed to do what they are told to do. Sarah scolded Hagar for not minding her. Hagar did not like to be scolded and she did not want to mind Sarah, so she ran away.

Hagar stopped to rest by a fountain of water. While she was resting, God spoke to her. He asked her where she had come from and where she was going. She said that she was running away from Sarah. God told her to go back and to mind Sarah. It was not right for her to run away.

Hagar went back and lived with Sarah and Abraham again. After a little while her little boy came and Abraham named him Ishmael. Ishmael means, "God hears." God had heard Hagar and had seen her when she was running away from Sarah.

QUESTIONS

1. What did Abraham and Sarah want that they did not have?
2. Who told them that he would give them a son?
3. What was the name of Sarah's servant?
4. What did Sarah say she would do?
5. Was it good for a man to have more than one wife?
6. What did Hagar begin to think when she knew that she was going to have a baby?
7. What did Sarah do to Hagar?
8. What did Hagar do?
9. Who spoke to Hagar when she stopped by the fountain of water?
10. What did God tell her to do?
11. What did Abraham name the little baby?
12. What does Ishmael mean?

Abraham and the Angels
(Gen. 18:1-15)

Abraham was nearly a hundred years old and Sarah was nearly ninety years old. One day God came to Abraham and told him that Sarah was going to have a little baby boy. Abraham was so surprised that he fell on his face and laughed. He said, "Can we have a child when I am a hundred years old and Sarah is ninety?"

One day Abraham was sitting out by the oak tree in front of his tent. He looked up and saw three men standing near him. They were really angels, but they looked like men. When Abraham saw them, he ran to them and bowed down to the ground. He told them to come in and eat with him. He told them to wash their feet and to rest under the tree. He ran into the tent and told

Sarah to make some bread very quickly. He then ran out to the field and got a calf that was young and good. He gave it to a servant to dress and cook. When everything was ready, he brought the calf and the bread and milk and butter to the angels for them to eat. He stood by them under the tree while they ate.

They said to him. "Where is Sarah, your wife?" Abraham said, "She is in the tent." One of the angels said, "I will come back about this time next year, and Sarah shall have a son."

Now, Sarah was listening behind them in the tent door and heard all that the angels said. She laughed and said, "Can I have a child when I am old?"

The angel heard Sarah laugh and he said, "Why did Sarah laugh?" Sarah was afraid because he had heard her.

She said, "I did not laugh." The angel said, "Yes, you did laugh." He knew she thought she was too old to have a child. He said, "Is anything too hard for the Lord?"

QUESTIONS

1. How old were Abraham and Sarah?
2. What did God tell Abraham?
3. What did Abraham do?
4. Whom did Abraham see one day when he was sitting in front of his tent?
5. Were they really men?
6. What did Abraham do when he saw them?
7. What did he say to them?
8. What did he bring them to eat?
9. What good news did the angels bring?
10. Who was listening in the door?
11. What did Sarah do?
12. Why did she say she did not laugh?
13. Why did she think she could not have a child?
14. What did the angel say?

The Bad News About Sodom
(Gen. 13:1-13; 18:16-33)

You remember that the servants of Lot and the servants of Abraham had a quarrel because there was not enough grass and water for all their sheep and cows. Abraham told Lot that it was not right to quarrel. The land was big, so he told Lot to pick out the part he wanted and move away, and they would not live together any more. Lot took the best part and moved away into the new part of the land. You remember that there was a very wicked city called Sodom near the place where Lot took his servants and his sheep.

Before long Lot took his family and moved into that very wicked city. That was a very bad thing to do. He was a good man and he did not like the things that the people in Sodom did. His family was not as good as he was and they did like to live in Sodom. His children liked the people and his girls wanted to marry the boys in the city. Some of them may have married the wicked people.

One day the angel of God told Abraham some very bad news. He said that God was going to destroy the wicked city of Sodom and all the people in it. That made Abraham feel very, very sad because he knew that Lot was there in the city. He loved Lot. He did not think that God would destroy the good people with the bad people because he thought that would not be right. He said, "Shall not the Judge of all the earth do right?" God is the Judge of all the earth. Abraham asked the angel if God would destroy the city if he could find fifty good people in it. The angel said that

God would save the whole city if he could find just a few good people in it. He said God would save the whole city if there were just ten good people in it.

There were not ten good people in the whole big city. God said he would have to destroy it. He said he would rain down fire from Heaven and burn everything in the city.

God did not want to destroy even a few good people with the bad. He sent two angels down to tell Lot what was going to happen and to tell him to run away from the city before the fire came so he would not be hurt. In our next story we will learn about the angels' visit to Lot's house.

QUESTIONS

1. Why did the servants of Lot and the servants of Abraham quarrel?
2. What did Abraham tell Lot to do?
3. What part of the land did Lot take when he left Abraham?
4. What was the name of the wicked city near him?
5. Where did Lot and his family move?
6. What bad news did the angels tell Abraham?
7. Why was Abraham sad?
8. For how many good people did God say he would save the whole city?
9. Could they find ten good people?
11. Whom did God send to tell Lot what was going to happen?
12. What were the angels going to tell Lot to do?

The Visit of the Angels
(Gen. 19:1-29)

The two angels came to Sodom late in the evening. Lot was sitting at the gate of the city, and he saw them coming. He ran to them and bowed down his head. He asked them to come into his house. He said they could spend the night with him and then get up early next morning and go on their way. He did not know that they were angels. They looked just like men. Lot was a good man and he was kind to strangers who came into the city and needed to stay all night. The angels said they could sleep in the street that night. Lot did not want them to do that He begged them to come into his house. They came in and he made a big dinner for them.

That night the wicked men of the city

came to Lot's house and wanted to hurt the strangers that had come. They did not know that they were angels. Lot went out and told them it was not right to hurt the men. He shut the door tight. The wicked men tried to hurt Lot, and they tried to break the door down. The angels reached out the door and pulled Lot into the house. Then they made all the wicked men go blind so they could not find their way. The wicked men stumbled and worried over trying to find their way to their own homes.

The angels told Lot that God was going to destroy the city because it was so wicked. They told him to take his family and run away before the fire came from Heaven to burn up the city. Lot went out and talked with the young men who had married his girls or who wanted to marry his girls. He told them

what the angels said. They laughed at him because they did not believe what he said. They did not want to leave the city.

Early the next morning the angels told Lot to take his wife and his two girls who were in the house and hurry away. Lot did not want to hurry because he was sorry to leave all the things he had in the city. The angels took hold of his hand and led them all out of the city because God was good to them. When they were outside the city, the angels told them to hurry to the mountains and not to look back.

As they were hurrying away, Lot's wife looked back. She turned to a pillar of salt. God said for them not to look back, and she did not mind him. Lot and his two girls ran away to the mountains and they lived there.

Lot was a very rich man when he lived with Abraham, but he went away to the wicked city. Then he had to run away and leave everything that he had. He was then a very poor man.

God rained down fire from heaven and burned up the city of Sodom and some other wicked cities around. When Abraham looked and saw the smoke from the cities, he was very sad.

QUESTIONS

1. Where was Lot when the angels came to the city?
2. What did Lot do when he saw the angels?
3. Where did the angels say they could sleep?
4. What did the wicked men of the city do that night?
5. What did the angels do to the wicked men?
6. What did the angels tell Lot that God was going to do?
7. What did they tell Lot to do?
8. Why did Lot not want to hurry away from the city?
9. How did the angels make Lot leave?
10. Where did they tell Lot and his family to go?
11. What did they tell them not to do?
12. Who looked back?
13. What happened to her?
14. How did God destroy the city?

Isaac and Ishmael
(Gen. 21:1-21)

God remembered the promise that he had made to Abraham and Sarah. He had said that they would have a little baby boy. At the very time that the angel had said, Sarah had a little boy. She named him Isaac, and that means laughter or laughing. She said, "God has made me laugh, and everybody who hears about it will laugh, too." You remember that she laughed when she was standing in the door of the tent and heard the angels tell Abraham that she would have a baby. She was so surprised. Abraham was one hundred years and Sarah was ninety years old.

The little child Isaac grew, and Abraham and Sarah loved him very much. One day Abraham made a feast because he was so proud of his little boy. A feast is a big, big dinner.

You remember that Abraham had another boy named Ishmael. His mother was Hagar, Sarah's servant. Ishmael did not like the little boy Isaac, and he made fun of him.

When they were having the feast because they were proud of Isaac, Sarah saw Ishmael making fun of her little boy. It made her very angry. She went and told Abraham that Ishmael and his mother could not live there any more. She did not want Ishmael to be with Isaac.

It made Abraham very sad because he loved Ishmael, too. He went and talked with God about it. God told him to send Ishmael and his mother away and let them live in another place.

Early the next morning Abraham

gave Hagar and Ishmael some bread and water and told them to go away to another place. They left, but they did not know where to go. They went out where no one lived and stayed until their food and water were gone. Ishmael wanted some water so badly that Hagar thought he was going to die. She laid him down by a little bush and went away where she could not see him. She sat down and cried.

God heard her crying, and he sent an angel to talk to her. The angel said, "Hagar, what is the matter?" Then he told her not to be afraid because God had heard her and he had heard her little boy, too. He told her to take up her little boy and hold him in her arms. When she did, she looked and saw a whole well of water not far away. She ran and filled a bottle with water and

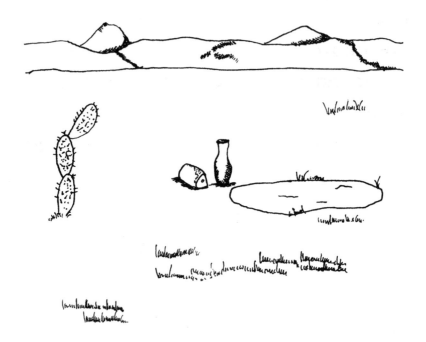

gave Ishmael a drink.

Ishmael grew to be a very strong man. He learned to hunt with bow and arrows. God took care of him.

QUESTIONS

1. What did God promise to Abraham and Sarah?
2. What did they name their little boy?
3. What did his name mean?
4. What did Sarah say?
5. How old were Abraham and Sarah when Isaac was born?
6. What did Abraham make because he was proud of his little boy?
7. What was the name of Abraham's other boy?
8. What did Ishamel do?
9. What did Sarah tell Abraham to do?
10. What did Abraham give Hagar and Ishmael when he sent them away?
11. Where did Hagar and Ishamel go?
12. Why was Ishmael about to die?
13. Who heard Hagar and Ishmael?
14. What did the angel say to Hagar?
15. What did Hagar see when she took up her little boy and looked around?
16. Who took care of them?

Abraham Offers Isaac
(Gen. 22:1-19)

In the days when Abraham lived, people did not worship God the way we do now. They had to build an altar out of rocks and kill a goat or cow or sheep and burn it on the altar. God would smell the smoke from the altar and know that the people loved him and were worshipping him.

Abraham loved God very much. He built an altar where he lived and burned an animal on it just the way God told him to do. God loved Abraham and gave him many good things because he worshipped him in the right way.

Abraham loved Isaac, his little boy, very, very much. He loved him so much that God was afraid he might love Isaac more than he loved God. One day God told him to do a very hard thing. He told him to take his little boy whom he loved so much and go up on the mountain and offer him as a sacrifice to God. That meant for him to kill him and burn him on the altar. Abraham had always obeyed God, so he got up early the next morning. He took two of his servants and Isaac and started up the mountain. He took some wood and some fire with him. On the way Isaac said, "Father, here is the wood and the fire, but where is the lamb for the sacrifice?" Abraham said, "God will provide himself the lamb for the offering." That meant that God would give them a lamb to use as a sacrifice.

Abraham told the servants to stop on the side of the mountain and wait for him and Isaac. He said, "We will worship and come again to you." The servants stopped and waited. Abraham

and Isaac went up on the mountain to the place God had told them.

When they were at the right place, Abraham built an altar. He tied Isaac's hands and his feet. Then he put him on the altar. He took his knife and reached out his hand to kill him. Just then the angel of God called to him and said, "Don't kill your little boy!" He said that now God knew that Abraham loved God better than he loved Isaac. He had been ready to kill his own little boy if God wanted him to.

Abraham took Isaac off the altar and he was not hurt at all. He looked around. There was a big sheep caught in the bushes by his horns. Abraham took the sheep and put him on the altar. He offered the sheep as a sacrifice to God instead of his little boy.

God said he would bless Abraham

and he would bless Isaac. That means
he would give them many good things.
God always blesses people who love
him.

QUESTIONS

1. How did Abraham worship God?
2. What was the name of Abraham's little boy?
3. How much did Abraham love him?
4. What hard thing did God tell Abraham to do?
5. What did Isaac ask Abraham on the way?
6. What did Abraham tell him?
7. What did Abraham tell the servants to do?
8. When Abraham built the altar what did he do to Isaac?
9. What was he about to do with his knife?
10. Who called to Abraham?
11. What did the angel say?
12. What did God know now?
13. What did Abraham see in the bushes?
14. What did God say he would do because Abraham loved him?

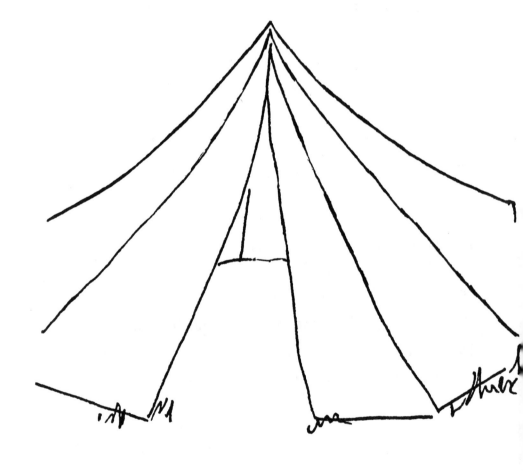

The Death of Sarah
(Gen. 23:1-20)

Abraham did not live in houses the way we do. He lived in tents, and he moved his tents from one place to another. He looked for the best grass and water for his sheep and cows. He lived in the land of Canaan. God told him that some day his children and his children's children could have all that land for their very own. Abraham could live anywhere he wanted to, but none of the land really belonged to him.

Abraham was a very old man now and his wife was very old, too. Isaac was a grown man. They had lots of cows and sheep and they had lots of servants. They were very rich.

The time came for Sarah to die because she was so old. When she died Abraham and Isaac were very, very sad. They cried and cried. Abraham wanted a good place to bury Sarah. He went to the people who lived near him and told them that he wanted a place to bury Sarah. Now, the people liked Abraham because they knew that God was with him. They told him that he could bury Sarah with their dead people wherever he wanted to. They said he could have the very best place, but Abraham wanted a place all his own. He asked one of the men to sell him a field that had a cave in it. A cave is a good place to bury some one, and the people often used one that way.

The cave that Abraham wanted was a big one and it was a good one. The name of it was Machpelah. The man who owned the cave said he would give it to Abraham, and he did not want to take any money for it. Abraham said

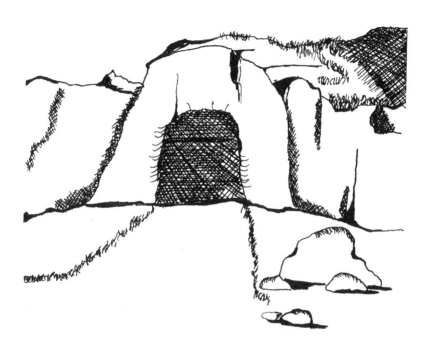

that would not be the right thing to do because it was a good cave and a good field. Abraham gave the man some money, and then the cave and the field belonged to Abraham.

He took Sarah and buried her in the cave of Machpelah. The cave belonged

to Abraham, and it would belong to
Isaac when Abraham was dead. It
would be a good place to bury many
other people of Abraham's family.

QUESTIONS

1. Where did Abraham live?
2. Why did he have to move so often?
3. Did the land belong to Abraham?
4. What did Abraham have to make him rich?
5. What happened to Sarah?
6. What did Abraham and Isaac do when she died?
7. What did Abraham need?
8. To whom did he go to ask about a place to bury Sarah?
9. What did the people tell him?
10. Did Abraham want to bury Sarah with the other dead people?
11. What kind of place did Abraham want?
12. What was the name of the cave which he bought?

The Servant at the Well
(Gen. 24:1-27)

One day Abraham called his best servant to him and said, "I do not want Isaac to marry one of the girls who live in this land. I want you to go back to the country where my people live and pick out a wife for him from my own kinsfolk.

The servant said, "What must I do if the woman I find will not come with me to be Isaac's wife?"

Abraham said, "God led me away from my father's house and away from my country and brought me into this land. He has promised to give this land to my children and my children's children. Now he will send his angel with you and help you find a wife for Isaac."

The servant promised to find the right woman from among Abraham's

kinsfolk. He began to get ready to make the trip. He took ten camels and lots of presents. He would have nice things to give to the woman he would find. He left Abraham and went to the city where Abraham's brother lived. He got there late in the evening. He stopped to rest just outside the city at a well. It was just the time for the women who lived in the city to go to the well to draw water.

The servant stood by the well and prayed to God. He asked God to send a girl down to the well and let her be the one he was wanting for a wife for Isaac.

While he was praying, a girl named
Rebekah came to the well to draw
water. Rebekah was Isaac's cousin. The

servant said, "Give me a drink." She said, "You may have a drink, and I will draw water for your camels, too." She hurried and gave the servant a drink, and she drew water for the camels. She gave them all they wanted to drink.

The servant asked her name and where she lived. When he learned that she was kin to Abraham, he knew that she was the girl he was looking for. He gave her some of the presents he had brought. He gave her a gold ring and two gold bracelets. She asked him to go home with her and spend the night with her family. She ran ahead and told her brother Laban about the servant at the well.

Laban saw the gold ring and the gold bracelets, so he ran to the well. He told the servant to come to his house and eat food and sleep. The servant was very happy that he had found the kinsfolk of Abraham. He bowed his head and worshipped God. He said, "Blessed be the Lord God of my master Abraham."

QUESTIONS

1. What did Abraham want his servant to do?
2. Whom did Abraham say God would send with the Servant?
3. What did the servant take with him?
4. Where did the servant stop to rest?
5. When he prayed, what did he ask God to do?
6. Who came to the well to draw water?
7. What did the servant say to her?
8. What did she say she would do?
9. What did he give her?
10. What did she ask him to do?
11. Who ran to the well to meet the servant?
12. What did the servant do because he was happy?

The Marriage of Isaac
(Gen. 24:28-67)

The servant of Abraham went into the house where Rebekah and her family lived. They gave his camels food and water and gave them a place to stay for the night. They gave the servant water to wash his feet. They gave him food to eat, but he said, "I will not eat until I have told you why I have come."

He told them about Abraham and about Sarah. He told them about Isaac. He said, "Abraham is a very rich man and he is very old. He is going to give everything he has to Isaac." He told them that Abraham did not want Isaac to marry a girl who lived in the land with them. He had sent his servant to pick out a girl from Abraham's kinsfolk to be a wife for Isaac. He told then how he stopped at the well and prayed to God to send the right girl. He told them that Rebekah came to the well to draw water while he was praying. He said that she gave him a drink and drew water for his camels. He then asked if they were willing for Rebekah to go home with him and to be Isaac's wife.

Rebekah's father and brother said, "This thing is from God, and we can not say anything about it." They said that Rebekah could go. The servant was so happy that he bowed down his head and worshipped God. He gave many pretty gifts to Rebekah and her mother and to her brother and her father.

Early the next morning the servant said he must go back home. He wanted Rebekah to go with him. Her family was sorry because they wanted her to wait a few days. They said, "Let her stay just ten days." The servant said he was in a hurry and he could not wait. They called Rebekah and asked her if she wanted to go. She said, "I will go."

They gave Rebekah a nurse to go with her. Rebekah and her nurse and the servant all started on their way. They were riding on the camels. When they were nearly to the place where Abraham lived, Rebekah looked up and saw some one walking in the field. She said, "Who is the man walking in the field to meet us?" The servant said, "It is my master." It was Isaac. Isaac was Rebekah's cousin, but she had never seen him before. Now she had come to be his wife.

Rebekah jumped down from her camel and put a veil over her face. Isaac came and took her to be his wife. He

106

took her to live in his mother's tent. He loved her, and he was not sad over his mother's death any more.

QUESTIONS

1. Where did Abraham's servant spend the night?
2. What did he want to tell them before he ate?
3. Can you tell the story about the servant at the well?
4. What did the servant want Rebekah to do?
5. Did the family say that Rebekah could go?
6. What did the servant do because he was so happy?
7. What did he give to Rebekah and her family?
8. How long did the family want Rebekah to stay with them?
9. What did she say when they asked her if she would go?
10. Who went with Rebekah?
11. Whom did they see walking in the field?
12. Where did Isaac take Rebekah to live?

The Famine in Canaan
(Gen. 26:1-11)

When Abraham was very, very old, the time came for him to die. His two sons, Isaac and Ishmael, took his body and buried it in the cave of Machpelah. That was the place where Sarah was buried.

Isaac and his wife Rebekah lived in the land of Canaan where Abraham had lived. They had to move from one place to another in the land just as Abraham had done because Isaac kept sheep and cows. He always wanted the best grass and water for them.

Before long there came a famine in

the land. A famine comes when it does not rain for a long time. Then the grass will not grow and the water goes dry. The sheep and cows were hungry and they wanted water. Isaac and his family were hungry, too. They thought they would have to leave the land and go to another land where there was plenty of food. They thought they could go to Egypt, but God spoke to Isaac and told him not to go to Egypt. He said, "Stay in this land and I will be with you and bless you." He told him to go to the edge of the land of Canaan where other people lived and where there was plenty of food. God told Isaac not to leave the land of Canaan because he was going to give him all that land. It was to be his and his children's as long as they lived.

Isaac moved to a place at the edge of

the land of Canaan called Gerar. When he got there, the men of the city asked him about Rebekah. He said, "She is my sister." He was afraid to say that she was his wife. He was afraid some one would kill him and take her because she was very pretty.

One day the king looked out his window and saw Isaac loving Rebekah. He called Isaac and said, "She is your wife. Why did you tell me that she was your sister?" Isaac said, "I was afraid some one would kill me." The king said that Isaac had done wrong because some one might have wanted to marry Rebekah. Then Isaac would have made some one else do wrong.

The king told all his people not to hurt Isaac or Rebekah. He said if anybody hurt them, he would be put to death.

QUESTIONS

1. What happened when Abraham was very old?
2. Where was he buried?
3. Where did Isaac and Rebekah live?
4. Why did they think they would have to leave the land?
5. Where did God tell them to stay?
6. What did God say he would do if they stayed in Canaan?
7. What did Isaac tell the people in Gerar about Rebekah?
8. Why did he tell a story?
9. What did the king see when he looked out the window?
10. What did he say to Isaac?
11. Was it right for Isaac to tell a story?
12. What did the king tell all his people?

Isaac and the Wells
(Gen. 26:12-33)

Isaac lived in Gerar for a long time. He planted things and raised very, very good crops. God loved him and gave him many good things so that he became very rich. He became richer than any of the people around him. He had lots of sheep, lots of cows, and lots of servants. He was so rich that the people who lived around him began to be jealous. They did not want him to have so many good things. They wanted the things for themselves.

One day the king of Gerar came to Isaac and said, "Go away from us because you are greater than we are." So Isaac left Gerar and went to live in the valley not far away.

Isaac was living in the land of Canaan where Abraham had been living. In some of the places where he moved, there were not any springs or rivers where he could get water for his sheep and cows. He had to dig wells in those places to get water. Abraham had dug some wells in the land, but the wicked people had filled them up so they could not be used any more. Isaac cleaned out one of the wells that Abraham had dug. When it was clean, the wicked people came and said, "This is our well." Isaac knew it was not their well because Abraham had dug it, but he did not quarrel with them. He knew it was not right to quarrel. He took his sheep and cows and moved to another place.

In the new place he cleaned out another well that Abraham had dug. This time the wicked people came again and said, "This is our well." Isaac did not quarrel with them. He took everything he had and moved again. He kept moving and digging wells until he came to one place where the wicked people did not bother him. He said, "Now God has made room for us."

One night God came to Isaac in a dream and said, "I am the God of Abraham, your father: do not be afraid. I will be with you and bless you." He said he would give Isaac some children, and 'he would give his children some children until there would be many, many of his people in the land. Isaac built an altar and worshipped God to show that he loved him.

QUESTIONS

1. What did Isaac have to make him rich?
2. Why did the people around him become jealous?
3. What did the king tell Isaac?
4. Who had lived in the land of Canaan before Isaac?
5. How did they get water when there were no springs or rivers?
6. What did the wicked people do to Abraham's wells?
7. What did Isaac do to some of the wells?
8. **What did the wicked people say?**
9. What did he do every time the wicked people wanted his well?
10. What did he say when the people did not bother him any more?
11. What did God say to Isaac one night?
12. What did Isaac do to show that he loved God?

Jacob and Esau
(Gen. 25:19-34)

When Isaac was nearly sixty years old, he became very sad because he and Rebekah did not have any little children. He prayed to God and asked him to give them some children. God had already promised that he would give them some children, so he gave them two little boys. They named them Esau and Jacob. Esau was a little older than Jacob, but Jacob was better than Esau. God loved Jacob better than he loved Esau.

In those days the oldest boy in the family was supposed to get two times as much of the things that the father had as the other boys when the father died. He got the best blessing. It was called the birthright. Esau was older than Jacob and he was supposed to get two times as much of the things that Isaac had as Jacob did. Esau was not a good man when he grew up, and he did not care about the birthright.

Esau was a hunter and he liked to stay in the fields and hunt animals. Jacob was a quiet man and he liked to stay at home in the tents. He kept sheep and cared for them. Isaac loved Esau more than he did Jacob because he liked to eat the meat that Esau brought him. Rebekah loved Jacob more than she did Esau because he stayed at home.

One day Esau had been hunting for a long time. He had not caught anything to eat. He became very hungry. He went back home, and Jacob had just cooked a pot of food that looked very good. Esau asked him to give him something to eat. Jacob said he would give him something to eat if Esau would let him have the birthright or best blessing. Esau said, "I am about to die, so it will not do me any good anyway. You may have it." Then Jacob gave him the food to eat. Esau ate all he wanted and did not care that he had given away his blessing.

When Esau was forty years old, he married two of the girls who lived in the land near him. This made Isaac and Rebekah very sad because the people near them were not good and they did not love God. They did not want their sons to marry girls who did not love God.

QUESTIONS

1. Why did Isaac become sad?
2. What did he ask God to do?
3. Name the two little boys.
4. What was the oldest boy in the family supposed to get?
5. What was the best blessing called?
6. What kind of work did Esau do when he grew up?
7. What kind did Jacob do?
8. Which one of the boys did Isaac love more?
9. Which one did Rebekah love more?
10. What did Esau want one day when he had been hunting?
11. What did Jacob say Esau must do before he could have something to eat?
12. Did Esau care that he had given away his birthright?
13. What did Esau do when he was forty years old?
14. Why did Isaac and Rebekah not like this?

Jacob Deceives His Father
(Gen. 27:1-45)

When Isaac was old, he became blind so that he could not see. He thought that the time was nearly come for him to die.

One day he called Esau to him and said, "I am old and I do not know when

I shall die. Go to the field and hunt venison and make some good meat for me to eat. When you come back, I will give you the best blessing."

Rebekah heard what Isaac told Esau. She wanted Jacob to have the best blessing. She called Jacob and told him to run out to the flock of goats and bring her two little goats. She said she would cook them and make them taste like the wild meat that Esau was hunting. She said that Jacob could take the meat to Isaac and he could get the best blessing. Jacob said, "My father will know that I am not Esau. Esau is a hairy man and I am smooth." Isaac could not see, so Jacob thought he would want to feel of his hands. Esau's hands were hairy. Rebekah told him to go ahead and get the little goats. She said she would help him make Isaac

think he was Esau.

Jacob ran out and got the two little goats. Rebekah cooked them just the way Isaac liked. When they were all ready, she got some of Esau's clothes that he had left at home. They smelled like the fields. She told Jacob to put them on. She took some of the goat's hair and put it on Jacob's hands and on his neck to make him feel like Esau. She gave him the meat and some bread, and he took them to his father.

When he came near his father, Jacob said, "Father, I have done what you told me to do." Isaac said, "Who are you, my son?" Jacob said, "I am Esau." Isaac said, "Come and let me feel your hands and see if you are Esau." When he felt the goat's hair on Jacob's hands he thought he was Esau. He said, "The voice is Jacob's voice,

but the hands are the hands of Esau."
He sounded like Jacob, but he felt like
Esau. Isaac thought he was Esau. He
ate the meat that Jacob had brought
and he blessed him. He promised him
many good things.

After a little while Esau came in from
hunting. He learned what Jacob had
done. He was very angry. He went to
his father and begged him to give him a
blessing, too. Isaac was very sad when
he heard what had happened and that
Jacob had told him a story. He had already promised Jacob all the good
things. He could not take them back.
Esau cried and cried. He was very
angry. He said he was going to kill
Jacob. He said it would not be long
until Isaac would die because he was
very old. As soon as his father was dead
he was going to kill Jacob.

QUESTIONS

1. What happened to Isaac when he was old?
2. What did he tell Esau to do?
3. Who heard him?
4. What did Rebekah tell Jacob to do?
5. How did Jacob say Isaac would know that he was not Esau?
6. Whose clothes did Rebekah put on Jacob?
7. What did she put on his hands and neck?
8. What did Jacob say to Isaac when he took the meat to him?
9. What did Jacob say when Isaac said, "Who are you?"
10. What did Isaac say when he felt of Jacob's hands?
11. Did Isaac give Jacob the blessing?
12. What did Esau do when he came in from hunting?
13. What did he say he was going to do to Jacob?
14. When did he say he would kill Jacob?

Jacob Leaves Home
(Gen. 27:46 - 28:22)

Rebekah heard that Esau was angry with Jacob and wanted to kill him. She was very sad. She called Jacob and told him to go away from home and stay until Esau was not angry any more. She told him to go to her brother's house in Haran where she used to live.

Isaac did not know that Esau wanted to kill Jacob. Rebekah went and told him that she did not like the girls that lived in that land. She did not like the girls that Esau had married. She said she did not want Jacob to marry one of them. She wanted him to marry some one of her kinsfolk. Isaac did not like the girls around them either, and he did not want Jacob to marry one of them. He called Jacob and told him to go to the city of Haran and find a girl to be

his wife from among Rebekah's kins-folk.

Jacob left home and started on his way. It was a long way to go and he was alone. He walked and walked and the sun was going down. He picked a place in a field to spend the night. He lay down on the ground to go to sleep. He took a stone or rock and put it under his head because he did not have a pillow.

When Jacob was asleep, he had a dream. He dreamed that he saw a ladder that was so long it reached all the way from earth to heaven. The angels of God were going up and coming down the ladder. God was standing at the very top. He talked to Jacob. He said, "I am the God of Abraham and the God of Isaac." He told Jacob that he would give him and his children all the land of

Canaan. He promised to be with him wherever he went and to bring him back safely to his home.

Early the next morning Jacob waked up. He was afraid. He said, "Surely God is in this place and I did not know it." He took the stone that he had slept on and set it up like an altar. He did not have an animal to offer as a sacrifice, but he poured oil on the stone and worshipped God. He called the place "Bethel." That means "the house of God." He promised that if God would be with him and take care of him he would worship God again in that very place. He said he would give to God part of everything that he had.

Then Jacob went on his way toward Haran. That was the city where Rebekah's brother lived.

QUESTIONS

1. Why was Rebekah sad?
2. What did she tell Jacob to do?
3. What did Rebekah tell Isaac?
4. What did Isaac tell Jacob to do?
5. Where did Jacob spend the night?
6. What did he put under his head?
7. What did he see in his dream?
8. What was going up and coming down the ladder?
9. Who was at the top of the ladder?
10. What did God say to Jacob?
11. How did Jacob feel when he waked up?
12. What did he say?
13. What did he do with the stone?
14. What did he call the place?

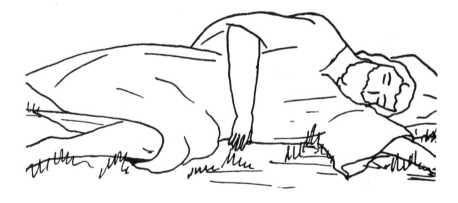

Jacob Meets Rachel
(Gen. 29:1-20)

Jacob walked and walked until he came to the city of Haran. He stopped to rest by a well where the people brought their sheep to get water. There were some men at the well with their sheep. Jacob asked them why they did not water their sheep and go away. They said they were waiting until all the other people brought their sheep and some one took away the stone from the top of the well. He asked them if they knew Laban, his mother's brother.

They said, "Yes, we know him." They said, "His daughter Rachel is coming now with her father's sheep."

When Jacob saw Rachel, he ran to the well and took away the stone from the top. He drew water for all her sheep. He then ran to her and kissed her. He told her that he was her cousin. He was very happy to find some of his kinsfolk. He cried. Rachel was happy to see her new cousin. She ran back to her house and told her father Laban. Laban ran to the well to meet Jacob. He kissed him. He told him to come to his house and spend the night.

Jacob was very glad to be at Laban's house. He stayed for a month. He helped do the work that Laban had to do. One day Laban said, "It is not right for you to work for me without pay even though you are kin to me." He asked

Jacob what pay he would like to have if he stayed and worked for him all the time.

Now Laban had two girls. One was named Leah and the other was Rachel. Leah was not pretty but Rachel was very pretty. Jacob loved Rachel. Jacob said to Laban, "I will work for you seven years if you will give me Rachel to be my wife."

Laban was pleased with Jacob. He said he would be glad to give Rachel to him if he worked seven years. He said he did not want her to marry a strange man. He wanted her to marry one of her kinsfolk.

Jacob stayed at Laban's house and worked seven years. It did not seem like a long time. He loved Rachel so much that the seven years seemed like only a few days.

QUESTIONS

1. Where did Jacob stop to rest in the city of Haran?
2. Who was at the well?
3. Why did they not go ahead and water their sheep?
4. Whom did they see coming to the well?
5. What did Jacob do when he saw Rachel?
6. Why did Jacob cry?
7. Whom did Rachel run to tell about Jacob?
8. What did Laban tell Jacob?
9. Name Laban's two girls.
10. Which one did Jacob love?
11. How long did Jacob say he would work for Rachel?
12. How long did the seven years seem?

Laban's Trick on Jacob
(Gen. 29:15-30)

Laban promised to give Jacob his daughter Rachel to be his wife if he would work for him seven years. Jacob did not mind the work because he loved Rachel so much. The seven years seemed like only a few days.

Finally the seven years were over. Jacob went to Laban and said, "I have worked seven years and now I want Rachel."

Laban made a big feast and invited all his friends to come to the wedding. He took Leah and put a veil on her face so Jacob could not see her face. He brought her to Jacob instead of Rachel.

When the wedding was over, all the friends went home. Leah took the veil off her face, and Jacob saw that she was not Rachel. Laban had played a trick on

him. Jacob was very angry because he had worked seven years for Rachel. He loved her. He did not love Leah. He went to Laban and said, "What have you done to me? I worked for you so that I could have Rachel. Why did you play this trick on me?"

Laban said, "It is not right to let the younger girl marry before the older girl does, so I had to let Leah marry first." Then he said, "I will give you Rachel if you will work for me another seven years." That was not fair, but Jacob did not quarrel about it. He wanted Rachel so much that he said he would work seven more years.

At last Jacob got Rachel to be his wife. He then had two wives. He loved Rachel but he did not love Leah. That made Leah very sad because she wanted Jacob to love her.

QUESTIONS

1. What did Laban promise to give to Jacob?
2. How long was Jacob to work for Rachel?
3. Why did the seven years seem so short?
4. What did Laban do to Leah?
5. How did Jacob feel when Leah took the veil off her face?
6. What did he say to Laban?
7. Why did Laban say he had played the trick?
8. How did Laban say that Jacob could get Rachel?
9. Why did Jacob say he would work another seven years?
10. Which one of his wives did Jacob love?

Jacob Wants to Go Home
(Gen. 29:31 - 31:21)

Jacob had married Leah and then Rachel. Soon Leah had some little children, but for a long time Rachel did not have any at all. She was sad. She had a servant whose name was Bilhah. She said she would give Bilhah to Jacob to be his wife. If Bilhah had a little child, Rachel would call it hers because Bilhah was her servant.

Leah did not like what Rachel had done. She had a servant whose name was Zilpah. She gave her to Jacob to be his wife. Now Jacob had four wives. He loved Rachel best of all.

Leah and the servant wives had lots of boys, and Leah had one girl. She named her Dinah. Rachel still did not have any children, and she was very, very sad. God saw that she was sad so he gave her a little boy. She named him Joseph. Jacob loved Joseph better than all his other boys because he was Rachel's son.

Jacob was still living with his uncle Laban and was working for him. Laban was not good to him. He did not want to pay him what was right for his work. He changed his pay ten times and sometimes treated him very bad.

One day Jacob said to Laban, "Let me go back to my old home where my father lives." Jacob was tired of working for Laban. Laban did not want him to go. He begged him to stay. God spoke to Jacob and said, "Go back to the land where your father lives and I will be with you."

Jacob did not tell Laban that God had spoken to him. He called Rachel and Leah out into the field where he could talk to them. He told them that he wanted to go back to his old home. Rachel and Leah said they were ready to go with him when ever he wanted to go.

Jacob did not tell Laban that he was going to leave. He knew that Laban would try to keep him from going. He gathered up all his things and took his wives and children and everything that he had. He put his wives and children on camels and started on his way. He slipped away before Laban knew he was going.

QUESTIONS

1. Why was Rachel sad?
2. What did she do so that she might have a little child?
3. What did Leah do?
4. How many wives did Jacob have now?
5. Which one did he love best?
6. What did God give to Rachel?
7. What did she name her little boy?
8. Why did Jacob love Joseph best of all?
9. Why did Jacob not want to work for Laban any more?
10. What did God say to Jacob?
11. Why did Jacob not tell Laban that he was leaving?
12. Whom did he tell?
13. What did Rachel and Leah say?
14. What did Jacob take with him?

Laban Follows Jacob
(Gen. 31:22-55)

Laban did not know that Jacob was going to leave. He had gone away from home when Jacob slipped away. Jacob had been gone three days when Laban came home. Laban was very angry. He wanted to kill Jacob. He took some of his men with him and began to run after Jacob.

He followed after Jacob for seven days. He was still very angry. Then God came to Laban in the night and said, "Don't you say anything good or bad to Jacob." Laban knew then that God was with Jacob and would not let him hurt him.

When Laban saw Jacob, he did not try to kill him. He said, "Why did you run away from my house without telling me? I would have made a feast for you. We would have had singing and dancing." Laban was not telling the truth, but he did not want Jacob to know that he was angry. He said, "I wanted to kiss my daughters and their children goodbye." He said that God came to him in the night and told him not to hurt Jacob.

Jacob told him that he had slipped away because he was afraid. He thought that Laban would not let him leave. He thought that he would not let him take Rachel and Leah away with him.

Laban said, "Why have you stolen my gods?" Laban worshipped idols. Idols are gods made out of wood or stone. It is not right to worship idols. Jacob did not worship idols. He had not stolen Laban's gods. He did not know anything about them. Somebody with him knew about them. Rachel had stolen them. She had them with her, but she had hidden them so that nobody could find them.

Jacob told Laban that he could look everywhere among their things and see if he could find them. Jacob did not know that they were there. Laban looked and looked. He could not find them. He went into Rachel's tent to look. She had hidden them and was sitting on them. She said she did not feel good so she could not get up. Laban looked all around and could not find his idols. He thought they were not there.

Jacob was angry with Laban for looking for them. He did not know that Rachel had them.

Laban promised not to hurt Jacob. He went back to his home. Jacob and his family went on their way back to his old home.

QUESTIONS

1. How long had Jacob been gone when Laban found out?
2. What did Laban want to do?
3. What did God say to Laban?
4. What did Laban say to Jacob when he caught up with him?
5. What did he saw he wanted to do?
6. What did Laban say that Jacob had stolen?
7. What kind of gods did Laban worship?
8. Who had stolen them?
9. Where did Laban look for them?
10. Why could he not find them?
11. How did Jacob feel when Laban could not find them?
12. What did Laban promise?

Jacob Is Afraid
(Gen. 32:1-23)

You remember that Jacob ran away from his father's house because his brother Esau wanted to kill him. Jacob had played a trick on Esau and he had told his father a story. He took the best blessing that his father was going to give to Esau. That made Esau very angry. He said he was going to kill Jacob. Jacob left everything he had and ran away from home. That was when he went to live with his uncle Laban.

Jacob had stayed with Laban a very, very long time. Now he had started back to his father's house. He had his four wives and all his little children with him. He had lots of cows and sheep with him, too. They could not go very fast.

Jacob was worried on the way. He

thought about Esau. He wondered if Esau would still be angry with him. He wondered if he would still want to kill him. He took some of his servants and told them to hurry on ahead and see Esau. He told them to come back and tell him if Esau was still angry with him. He wanted them to tell Esau that he had been living at Laban's house and that he was now on his way home with his wives and little children.

The servants left and went on ahead to find Esau. After a while they came back. They told Jacob that they found Esau and that he was coming to meet Jacob with four hundred men with him.

When Jacob heard that, he was very afraid. He thought that Esau was bringing all those men with him to kill him. He took his wives and children and his servants and put them in two groups. He said if Esau came and killed one group, maybe the other group could run away and not be killed. He put Rachel and her little boy Joseph in the safest place because he loved them best.

He prayed to God. He asked him to take care of him and not let Esau hurt him. He said that God had promised to do good to him and bless him, and now he was afraid of Esau. He asked God to keep Esau from killing him and his family.

Jacob and his family stopped to spend the night by a little river. In the next story we will learn something that happened that night. A strange thing happened to Jacob.

QUESTIONS

1. Why had Jacob run away from home?
2. What had Jacob done to make Esau angry?
3. Why was Jacob worried on his way home?
4. Whom did Jacob send ahead to see Esau?
5. What did the servants say when they came back?
6. What did Jacob think when he heard that Esau was coming to meet him?
7. Why did Jacob divide his family into two groups?
8. Where did he put Rachel and her little boy?
9. Whom did he ask to take care of him?
10. What had God promised?
11. What did he ask God to keep Esau from doing?
12. Where did Jacob and his family stop to spend the night?

Jacob and the Angel
(Gen. 32:24-32)

Jacob was afraid of his brother Esau. He had heard that he was coming to meet him with four hundred men. He thought that Esau wanted to kill him. He thought he would send a present to Esau. Maybe he would like the present and would not be angry any more.

He picked out some of his camels and some cows and some sheep and some goats and put each group by themselves. He gave the camels to one of his servants and told him to take them to Esau. As soon as the servant was gone, Jacob sent another servant with the cows. When that servant was gone, he sent still another servant with the sheep. When that servant was gone, he sent another servant with the goats. He told the servants to tell Esau that all those presents were from Jacob and that he was coming on behind.

Jacob had his wives and his children and his servants all divided into groups so that they would be safe. He let them cross the river, and he stayed alone on the other side. He wanted to pray to God because he was afraid of Esau.

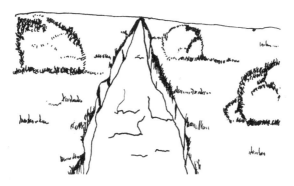

A very strange thing happened while Jacob was there alone. A man suddenly came and began to wrestle with him. It looked like a man, but it was really an angel. Jacob and the angel wrestled all night. When it began to be nearly morning, the angel touched Jacob's right hip and hurt it. Jacob could not walk then without limping. The angel said, "Let me go because it is nearly morning." Jacob said, "I will not let you go until you bless me." The angel said, "What is your name?" Jacob said, "My name is Jacob." The angel said, "Your name shall be called no more Jacob but Israel."

Israel means "Prince of God," and that was a real good name. Jacob was glad to have the new name. We still call him Jacob, but we call his children "The children of Israel."

Jacob said he had seen God because he had seen his angel. He was not so afraid now since he had seen the angel. He knew that God would be with him. He went across the river to his wives and children, but he had to limp when he walked.

QUESTIONS

1. Why was Jacob afraid?
2. What did he want to send to Esau?
3. Name some of the animals he picked out to send to Esau.
4. Who carried the presents?
5. How did Jacob fix his family to make them safe?
6. When the family went across the river, why did Jacob stay on the other side?
7. Tell about the strange thing that happened that night.
8. When it was nearly morning, how did the angel hurt Jacob?
9. What new name did the angel give Jacob?
10. What does Israel mean?
11. Whom did Jacob say he had seen?
12. How did Jacob walk after he wrestled with the angel?

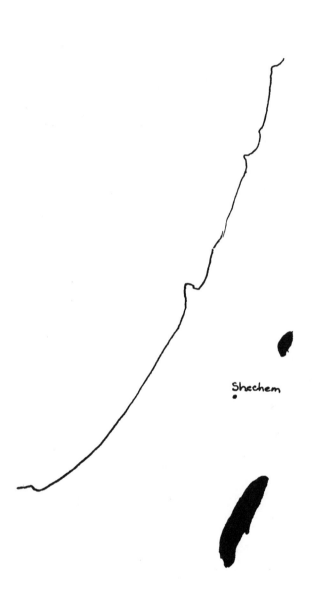

Shechem

Jacob Meets Esau
(Gen. 33:1-20)

Jacob looked up and saw Esau coming with four hundred men. He arranged his wives and children again to try to make them safe. He put Rachel and Joseph behind all the rest. He wanted them to be the safest because he loved them best of all.

He went on ahead of them. He bowed down to the ground seven times to show Esau that he was not angry with him. When he came near, Esau ran to him. He hugged and kissed him and cried. He was not angry any more. He was glad to see Jacob.

Esau looked all around and said, "Who are all these people you have with you?" Jacob told him that they were his wives and children that God had given to him.

Leah and Rachel and the two servant-wives came and bowed down before Esau. All the children came and bowed down before him, too.

Esau asked Jacob why he had sent all those presents to him. Jacob said he sent them so that Esau would be pleased with him. Esau said, "I have enough. You keep them for yourself." Jacob said, "No, I sent them to you and I want you to have them. I have enough without them." Jacob wanted to show how happy he was that Esau was not angry with him any more. He begged him to take the presents. At last Esau took them.

Esau said that he would stay with Jacob and help him carry his wives and children and all his things along the way. Jacob said, "We cannot go fast because the children are little, and the little calves and lambs are young." He told Esau to go on his way and he and his family would go along slowly. He knew the way. He did not want to go fast and hurt his little children and his little animals.

Esau left Jacob and went back to his own home. Jacob went on until he came to a place called Shechem. There he stopped and bought some land. He decided to live there. He built an altar to worship God.

QUESTIONS

1. Why did Jacob put Rachel and Joseph behind all the others?
2. What did Jacob do when he saw Esau?
3. What did Esau do?
4. What did Esau say when he saw all of Jacob's wives and children?
5. Who did Jacob say had given him his family?
6. What did Jacob's wives and children do?
7. What did Esau say about the presents Jacob had sent to him?
8. Why did Jacob beg Esau to keep them?
9. Why did Esau want to stay with Jacob?
10. Why did Jacob say he would have to go along slowly?
11. Where did Jacob stop to live?
12. What did he build there?

Dinah
(Gen. 34:1-31)

You remember that Jacob had lots of boys but only one girl. Her name was Dinah.

Jacob and his family lived at Shechem. It was a good place to live. They had room for their sheep and goats and cows. Jacob was a rich man, and the people of the city liked him.

Dinah went to visit the girls who lived in the city. She met a man whose name was Shechem. He had the same name as the city. Shechem fell in love with Dinah. He wanted her for his wife. He took her to his house.

When Jacob's boys heard about it, they were very angry. They did not want Dinah to marry a man in that land. The people there did not worship God. God wanted his people to marry others who worshipped him. Shechem begged Jacob to let him marry Dinah because he loved her. He said he would pay anything Jacob asked if only he could marry her. The men of the city

were pleased for Shechem to marry
Dinah. Jacob was rich. They thought if
he let his daughter marry Shechem they
might get some of the things he had.

Two of Jacob's sons learned that
Dinah was in Shechem's house. They
became very angry. They were so angry
that they did something very wrong.
They took their swords and went into
the city. They killed all the men in the
city. They killed Sehchem and his
father. They took all the sheep and
cows and all the good things they could
find that had belonged to the dead men.
They stole the wives and children of the
men and took them home to be servants. They went and took Dinah out of
Shechem's house and carried her back
to her home.

When Jacob heard what his boys had
done, he was very sad. He told them

that they had done wrong. He said they had made all the people around hate them. He said everybody would hear what they had done. They would all want to kill Jacob and his family. It was a very, very wicked thing to do.

Jacob had to take his family and leave Shechem. He was afraid to stay there any longer. He said all the people would hate him.

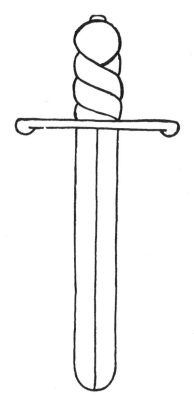

QUESTIONS

1. What was the name of Jacob's daughter?
2. Where did Jacob and his family live?
3. Whom did Dinah go to visit?
4. What was the name of the man she met?
5. What did Shechem do?
6. Why were Jacob's boys angry?
7. What did Shechem beg Jacob to do?
8. Why were the men of the city pleased?
9. What very wicked thing did two of Jacob's boys do?
10. What did they steal out of the city?
11. How did Jacob feel when he heard what his boys had done?
12. Why did Jacob move away from Shechem?

Jacob at Bethel
(Gen. 35:1-15)

God spoke to Jacob and told him to take his family and go up to Bethel to worship him. A long, long time ago when Jacob was running away from home when Esau wanted to kill him, he had stopped to rest at Bethel. It was there that he had the dream of the

ladder with the angels going up and coming down on it. When he had the dream, he promised God that he would worship him at Bethel if God would be with him and bring him home again safely.

God had been with him and had taken care of him. He had kept Esau from hurting him. He had brought him back safely to his old home. Now it was time for him to remember his promise and go to worship God at Bethel.

Jacob called his wives and all his family. He told them that God had spoken to him and told him to go up to Bethel to worship.

Jacob's wives and servants had some idol gods with them. You remember that Rachel had stolen Laban's gods when they left his house. It is wrong to worship idols.

Jacob told his family to bring him all their idol gods and all the things they could use to make more idols. They brought them all to Jacob, and he buried them under an oak tree. He wanted his family to worship the God in heaven and not to worship the idol gods that they had made.

They all went to Bethel and worshipped God. God spoke to Jacob and blessed him. He told him that he would be with him and take care of him. He said he would make his name great so that all people would know him. He promised to give him all the land of Canaan, and it was a very, very good land. He said that Jacob's children would have children. Their children would have children until there would be a great nation of his people. His children would be called by his new

name that the angel gave him. They would be called, "The children of Israel."

Then God went up from him in the place where he had talked to him. Jacob built an altar and worshipped.

QUESTIONS

1. What did God tell Jacob to do?
2. Tell about the dream that Jacob had.
3. What had Jacob promised God?
4. What did Jacob tell his family?
5. What did some of Jacob's family have that they should not have?
6. What did Jacob tell them to bring to him?
7. What did he do with the idol gods?
8. Whom did Jacob want his family to worship?
9. Where did they all go to worship God?
10. Who came and talked with Jacob?
11. Tell some of the things that God said.
12. What do we call Jacob's children?

Joseph's Dream
(Gen. 37:1-17)

Jacob had twelve boys, but he loved Joseph best of all. He made him a coat of many colors to show how much he loved him. Joseph was a good boy. He was better than all the other boys. Sometimes he would tell his father about the bad things that his brothers did. This made his brothers angry. They did not like him because he told on them when they did bad things.

They did not like him because his father loved him best of all.

Something else happened that made the brothers hate Joseph more than ever. He dreamed some dreams and told them to his brothers. He told them that he dreamed that they were all together in the field. They were tying up the bundles of grain that they had cut. His bundle stood straight up in the field. His brothers' bundles came and bowed down before it, and worshipped it. His brothers did not like the dream. They asked Joseph if he thought that some day he would rule over them and that they would bow down before him.

Joseph dreamed another dream. He dreamed that the sun and the moon and eleven stars bowed down and worshipped him. This time his father scolded him when he heard the dream. He said, "Shall I and your mother and your brothers all fall down and worship you?"

The brothers were jealous of him. They hated him more and more when they heard his dreams. They called him the Dreamer. His father thought and thought and wondered what the dreams meant. Joseph did not forget his dreams.

Jacob and his family lived in the land of Canaan. They kept sheep and cows and goats. They moved from place to place where they could find plenty of good grass and fresh water for the animals to eat. Sometimes the family all stayed in one place and the boys would take the animals and go from place to place with them looking for good grass and water. Sometimes the boys would be gone from home for a long time taking care of their sheep and cows.

QUESTIONS

1. How many boys did Jacob have?
2. Which one did he love best?
3. What did Jacob make for Joseph?
4. Why did the brothers hate Joseph?
5. Tell the dream that Joseph had about the bundles of grain.
6. Why did the brothers not like the dream?
7. Tell the dream about the sun and moon and stars.
8. Who scolded Joseph about that dream?
9. What did Joseph's brothers call him?
10. What did they ask Joseph?
11. Where did Jacob and his family live?
12. What kind of work did they do?

Joseph Is Sold
(Gen. 37:12-30)

Jacob's boys had been gone from home a long time taking care of their sheep and cows. Joseph stayed at home with his father.

One day Jacob called Joseph and told him to go and look for his brothers. He told him to see how they were getting along with their sheep and cows and come back and tell him.

Joseph started on his way. He

walked and walked. His brothers looked up and saw him coming. They said, "Here comes that Dreamer. Let's kill him." They said they would kill him and throw him in a pit. Then they would tell their father that a wild animal had killed him.

One of the boys, whose name was Reuben, heard what the other brothers had said. He did not want to kill him. He said, "Let's not kill him. Let us put him down in a pit and leave him." He thought that he would get him out and take him back home.

Joseph did not know what his brothers said. He came to them, and they caught hold of him. They took off his pretty coat of many colors. They put him down in the pit. There was no water in the pit, but it was deep. He could not get out. He begged and begged his brothers to take him out of the pit.

The brothers did not listen to Joseph. They sat down to eat. While they were eating, they looked up and saw a group of people coming. The people were traders. Traders buy and sell things. The boys ran to the pit. They took Joseph out of the pit and sold him to the traders. The traders paid them twenty pieces of money.

Reuben had gone away when the traders came by. He did not know what his brothers had done. After a while he came back to the pit and looked in. Joseph was gone. He was very sad. He tore his clothes to show how sad he was. He cried and cried. He did not want to hurt Joseph. He wanted to take him back home, and now it was too late.

QUESTIONS

1. Where were Jacob's boys?
2. Which one stayed at home?
3. What did Jacob tell Joseph to do?
4. When the brothers saw Joseph coming, what did they say?
5. What did they say they would tell their father?
6. What did Reuben tell them?
7. What did the brothers do when Joseph came to them?
8. Whom did the brothers see coming?
9. What did they do to Joseph then?
10. How much money did the traders pay them?
11. What did Reuben do when he found Joseph gone?
12. What had Reuben meant to do to Joseph?

Jacob Is Sad
(Gen. 37:31-36)

After the brothers had sold Joseph to the traders, they took his pretty coat of many colors and tore it into pieces. They killed a little goat and took the blood and dipped the coat in the blood. They all went back to their home and came to their father Jacob. They showed him the coat. They said, "We found this coat. Do you know if it is Joseph's coat?"

Jacob saw the coat that he had made. He knew that it was Joseph's coat. He said, "It is my son's coat. A wild animal has killed him." The brothers did not tell him what they had done.

Jacob had loved Joseph best of all his boys. Now he thought that he was dead. He was very, very sad. He tore his clothes to show how sad he was. He cried and cried. He said that he was never going to stop crying. He said he was going to cry the rest of his life until he died. His children tried to make him feel better, but he would not stop feeling sad.

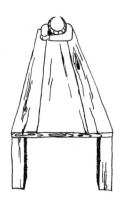

Joseph was not really dead. He had not been eaten up by a wild animal. His brothers had sold him to some traders. The traders bought Joseph to sell again as a slave. A slave is some one who has to work without any pay for his work. That was a bad thing to be.

The traders took Joseph a long way from his home. They took him to a country called Egypt. In Egypt they sold him to a man named Potiphar. Potiphar was an officer who helped to guard the king. He was an important man.

God knew what had happened to Joseph. He knew that he was in Egypt. He was with him to take care of him. He would not let anything hurt him while he was away from home.

QUESTIONS

1. What did the brothers do to Joseph's coat?
2. Where did they all go?
3. What did they say to their father?
4. What did Jacob say had happened to Joseph?
5. What did Jacob do?
6. How long did Jacob say he was going to be sad over Joseph?
7. What had really happened to Joseph?
8. Why did the traders buy Joseph?
9. Where did the traders take him?
10. To whom did they sell him?
11. Who knew what had happened to Joseph?
12. Who went down into Egypt with him?

Joseph in Potiphar's House
(Gen. 39:1-23)

Potiphar was an important man in the land of Egypt. He was an officer who helped to guard the king. He bought Joseph and brought him into his house to be his servant. God was with Joseph and Potiphar liked him. Everything that Joseph did turned out to be good. He was a good servant. He did everything he was told to do. Potiphar liked him so much that he made him head over all his servants and over everything in his house. God blessed Potiphar because he was good to Joseph. He gave him many good things.

Potiphar's wife was not a good woman. She began to watch Joseph every day as he went about his work. She tried to get him to do things that were not right. Joseph would not talk to her. He would not do anything that was wrong. She was very wicked. She kept on day after day trying to get Joseph to do wrong.

One day she told a story on Joseph. She told her husband that Joseph had tried to make love to her while Potiphar was away from home. Potiphar did not ask Joseph if he had done wrong. He thought his wife was telling the truth. He was very angry with Joseph. He was so angry that he would not let Joseph stay in his house any longer. He took him and put him in prison where the king put men who had done wicked things.

God saw Joseph when he was put in prison. He was kind to him. He knew that Joseph had not done anything wrong. He blessed Joseph and let the keeper of the prison like him.

The keeper of the prison saw that Joseph was a good man. He made him head over all the prisoners. The keeper did not look after anything in the prison because Joseph took care of everything for him. God made everything that Joseph did turn out good.

QUESTIONS

1. Who was Potiphar?
2. Why did he buy Joseph?
3. Who was with Joseph?
4. What did Potiphar do because he liked Joseph?
5. What did Potiphar's wife try to get Joseph to do?
6. What did she tell her husband one day?
7. How did Potiphar feel?
8. What did Potiphar do to Joseph?
9. Who knew what had happened to Joseph?
10. How did the keeper of the prison feel about Joseph?
11. What did he do with Joseph?
12. How did everything Joseph did turn out?

Joseph in Prison
(Gen. 40:1-23)

While Joseph was in prison a strange thing happened. The king became angry with two of his servants and put them in prison, too. One of them was his butler who was the chief servant in the house. The other was his baker who cooked his food. He put the two men in the prison where Joseph was. Joseph looked after them every day.

One morning Joseph found the two servants very sad. He asked them why they were sad. They said they had dreamed dreams that worried them. They did not know what the dreams meant. Joseph told them that only God could tell the meaning of dreams. He asked them to tell him their dreams.

The butler said he dreamed that he saw a vine that had three branches on

it. There were ripe grapes on the vine. He took the grapes and pressed the juice in his hands and gave the juice to the king.

God told Joseph what the dream meant. Joseph said, ''The three branches are three days. In three days the king will take you out of prison, and you will be his butler again.'' Then he said, ''When you get out of prison, tell the king about me so that he will let me out of prison, too.'' He told him that he had not done anything wrong. His brothers had sold him and Potiphar's wife had told a story on him. He did not need to be in prison.

The baker liked what Joseph had told the butler. He wanted to tell his dream, too. He said he dreamed that he had three baskets of food on his head. The birds came and ate the food out of the baskets.

Joseph said, "The three baskets are three days. In three days the king will take you out of prison and will hang you on a tree. You will die."

In three days the things happened just as Joseph had said. The king sent and took the butler out of prison and let him work for him again. He took the baker out of prison and put him to death.

Joseph had asked the butler to tell the king about him, but the butler forgot all about him. Joseph had to stay in prison two more years.

QUESTIONS

1. Who was put in prison with Joseph?
2. How did the two servants look one morning?
3. Why were they sad?
4. Who did Joseph say could tell the meaning of dreams?
5. Tell the butler's dream about the grapes.
6. What did Joseph say the dream meant?
7. What did Joseph tell the butler to say to the king?
8. Tell the baker's dream.
9. What did Joseph say his dream meant?
10. What did the king do to the butler in three days?
11. What did he do to the baker?
12. Why did the butler not tell the king about Joseph?

Pharaoh's Dreams
(Gen. 41:1-14)

Pharaoh was the king of Egypt. One night he had two dreams, and the dreams worried him. They were strange dreams and he did not know what they meant. In those days God sometimes told people things in dreams. He does not tell us things in dreams now. We have the Bible to tell us everything that God wants us to know.

Pharaoh dreamed that he was standing by the river. He saw seven cows come up out of the river. They were fat and nice looking. They came and ate the grass on the bank of the river. After a while seven more cows came up out of the river. These cows were poor and lean. They were very bad looking. Then a very strange thing happened. The poor, lean cows ate up the good fat cows. They were just as poor and lean as they were before they ate the fat cows.

Pharaoh awoke out of his sleep. He wondered what the dream meant. He went back to sleep and had another dream. In this dream he saw a stalk of corn grow up. On the stalk there came out seven big, fat ears of grain. After a while seven more ears came out of the stalk. These ears were poor and bad. Then a very strange thing happened. The poor, bad ears ate up the good, fat ears. They were just as poor and bad looking as they were before they ate the good ears.

The king awoke out of his sleep and he was troubled. He felt very bad because he did not know what the dreams meant. He called for all his wise men and told them his dreams. They thought and thought. They could not tell him what they meant.

The king's butler heard that the king was troubled over his dreams. He came to the king and said, "I remember something now that I had forgotten." He told about a young man that he had seen down in the prison. That young man was Joseph. The butler said Joseph could tell the meaning of dreams.

Pharaoh was pleased when he heard this, so he sent a man to call Joseph to come out of prison to tell him the meaning of his dreams. In our next story we will learn what the dreams meant.

QUESTIONS

1. Who was Pharaoh?
2. What happened to make him worried?
3. How did God sometimes talk to people in those days?
4. How does he talk to us now?
5. Tell Pharaoh's dream about the cows.
6. Tell his dream about the ears of corn.
7. Why did the king feel bad about his dreams?
8. Whom did he call to see if they could tell the meaning of the dreams?
9. Who heard about the king's dreams?
10. What did the butler remember?
11. Who did the butler say could tell the meaning of the dreams?
12. What did the king do?

Joseph Tells Pharaoh's Dream
(Gen. 41:14-42)

The king called for Joseph to come out of prison. Joseph was very glad. He had been in prison a long time and he had not done anything wrong. He put on clean clothes and shaved his face before he came to see the king. He was thirty years old when he came out of prison to see the king.

When Joseph came in, Pharaoh said, "I have had two dreams and they trouble me. I have heard that you can tell what dreams mean." Joseph said, "I cannot tell you but God can." He said that God would tell him and then he would tell the king.

Pharaoh told Joseph his dream about the seven bad cows that ate up the seven good, fat cows. He told him about the seven bad ears of corn that ate up the seven good ears. Joseph listened to the strange dreams. Then he said, "The two dreams mean the same thing." He said that God was telling Pharaoh something that was about to happen. The seven good cows and the seven good ears of corn meant seven good years when lots of food would grow in the land of Egypt. There would be so much food grown that the people could not use all of it. After a while there would come seven bad years when there would be a famine. A famine is a time when nothing will grow and when people get hungry.

Joseph said that Pharaoh had two dreams because God was sure this thing was going to happen. He wanted Pharaoh to know.

Joseph said for Pharaoh to pick out a wise man and set him over the land of

Egypt. He said for him to send men all over the land to gather up the part of the food that would grow that the people did not need. He said that they must build store houses and save all the food during the seven good years. Then when the seven bad years came they would have plenty of food stored up. The people of Egypt would have food to eat and would not be hungry.

Pharaoh and his servants were pleased with Joseph. They liked the things he said. They said he was a wise man. They saw that God was with him. Pharaoh said, "We cannot find a wiser man than Joseph. We will set him over the land of Egypt. We will do whatever he says." The king took off his ring and put it on Joseph's finger to show that he was a ruler.

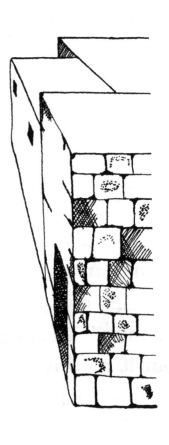

QUESTIONS

1. What did Joseph do before he went to see the king?
2. How old was Joseph?
3. What did Pharaoh tell Joseph?
4. Who did Joseph say could tell the meaning of dreams?
5. What did he say God was telling Pharaoh?
6. What did the seven good cows and the seven poor ears of corn mean?
8. What did Joseph tell Pharaoh to do?
9. What was the man to do whom Pharaoh picked out?
10. Why were they to gather up food and save it?
11. Who did Pharaoh say was the wisest man?
12. What did Pharaoh give to Joseph to show that he would be a ruler?

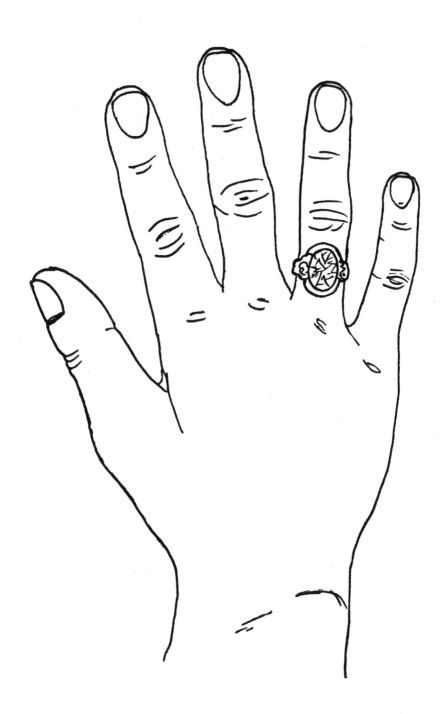

Joseph, the Ruler
(Gen. 41:42-53)

Do you remember that when Joseph was a little boy at home his father loved him best of all his children? He was a good boy. His brothers hated him because he was better than they were. They were jealous of him. They wanted to kill him, but they did not. They sold him to some traders who took him down into Egypt and sold him again. He was made a servant in Potiphar's house and he was the best servant there. Potiphar's wife told a story on him and tried to make him do wrong. He would not do wrong. Potiphar became angry with him and put him in prison. The keeper of the prison made him head over all the prisoners.

Joseph could tell the meaning of dreams because God was helping him.

He got to see the king, and he told the king the meaning of his dreams. In our last story he had been made the ruler over all the land of Egypt. He was over everybody except the king. He was a good ruler and all the people loved him. God made everything he did turn out to be good.

There came seven years when more things grew in the fields than the people could use. Joseph told the king that this would happen. Joseph and the men with him began to gather up all the food that the people did not need. They built store houses all over the land in which to put the extra food. At first they wrote down how much they gathered up. After a while there was so much that they could not count it. They built more store houses and more store houses. Soon all of them were full. They gathered up all the food for people and for animals. They did not let any of it go to waste. Joseph said there would come seven years when nothing would grow. They would need all that was stored up.

The king loved Joseph so much that he put his gold ring on his finger. He dressed him in fine clothes. He put a gold chain around his neck and let him ride in a fine chariot. He made all the people bow down before him. He said that nobody in all the land could do anything without asking Joseph. He found a good girl and gave her to Joseph to be his wife.

God was with Joseph. He saw everything he did. He made everything he did turn out for good.

QUESTIONS

1. Why did Joseph's brothers hate him?
2. What did they do to him?
3. In whose house was he a servant?
4. Why was he put in prison?
5. What did the keeper of the prison do to him?
6. Why did he get to see the king?
7. Who was helping Joseph all the time?
8. Who made him ruler over the land?
9. What did Joseph and his men do when more things grew than they could use?
10. Why did they gather up all the food and save it?
11. What did the king do to show that he loved Joseph?
12. Why did everything that Joseph did turn out to be good?

The Seven Bad Years Begin
(Gen. 41:54 - 42:6)

When the seven good years were over, there began to be seven bad years when nothing would grow. The people in Egypt soon used up all the food that they had in their houses. Nothing would grow in the fields. They began to be hungry. They went to Pharaoh and told him that their food was gone and they were hungry. Pharaoh said, "Go to Joseph. Do whatever he says."

Joseph opened the store houses where all the food was stored and began to sell food to the people.

The famine was not just in the land of Egypt. It was in all the countries round about. In the other countries they had not stored up food during the seven good years. They did not know about the seven bad years. They began to be hungry. They heard that there was plenty of food in the land of Egypt. All the people around began to come to the land of Egypt to buy food. Joseph sold food to all of them.

Joseph's father Jacob and his brothers lived in the land of Canaan. The famine was there, too, and they began to be hungry. One day Jacob heard that there was plenty of food in Egypt. He called his boys and told them to go to the land of Egypt and buy food.

Joseph had eleven brothers. The youngest boy was Benjamin. Jacob loved Benjamin best of all now because he thought Joseph was dead. He said that Benjamin could not go with all the brothers to Egypt to buy food. He was afraid something would happen to him. So Benjamin stayed at home with his father.

The ten brothers went down to Egypt to buy food. They came to Joseph because he was the one who sold the food. He went out to meet them, and he knew that they were his brothers. They did not know him. They did not know that he was in Egypt. He did not talk the way they did. He talked the way the people of Egypt talked. He dressed the way the people of Egypt dressed. His brothers could not understand what he said. Some one had to tell them what he said, but he knew what they said.

The brothers all bowed down before

Joseph. Joseph remembered the dreams he had when he was just a boy. Now they were coming true. His brothers were bowing down before him.

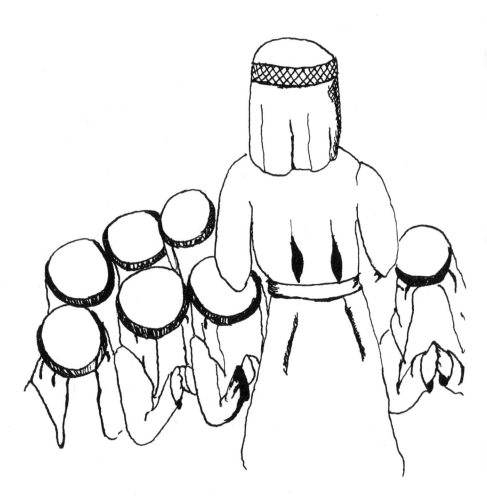

QUESTIONS

1. What happened when the seven good years were over?
2. When the people began to get hungry what did they do?
3. To whom did Pharaoh tell them to go?
4. What did Joseph do?
5. What was happening to people in other countries?
6. What did they do when they heard that there was plenty of food in Egypt?
7. What did Jacob tell his boys to do?
8. How many brothers did Joseph have?
9. What was the name of his youngest brother?
10. Why would Jacob not let Benjamin go with the other boys to Egypt?
11. What did the brothers do when they saw Joseph?
12. What did Joseph remember?

Joseph and His Brothers
(Gen. 42:7-38)

Joseph did not know if his brothers were good men now or if they would still hate him. He talked roughly to them and treated them badly. He did not hate them. He wanted to see what kind of men they were. He said they had come down to see how bad the land looked when nothing would grow. He said they wanted to make war on his people.

The brothers were not wicked men. They were sorry now for what they had done to Joseph. They told him that they had not come down to make war. They had come to buy food. They said they were all brothers. They said they had one more brother at home and that one of their brothers was dead. It was Joseph that they thought was dead.

They said their father was still living and that he was at home with their youngest brother. Joseph acted as if he did not believe what they said. He said he would send one of them back to get the other brother to see if they were telling the truth.

He put them all in prison and kept them for three days. He told them that they could all go home except one. He would keep one of them in prison to be sure that the others would come back. He told them that they could not see his face again unless they brought their youngest brother back with them.

Joseph gave them sacks of food to carry home. They paid him money for the food and started home. On the way home they stopped to feed the animals they were riding on. They looked in their sacks. There was the money they

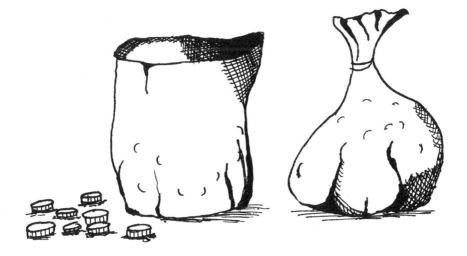

had paid. They were very afraid. They did not know what had happened.

When they got home they told Jacob all that had happened. They told about the ruler who talked roughly to them and treated them badly. They told him that one of the boys had to stay in prison. They told how they had found the money in their sacks on the way home. They were very afraid. They told him that the ruler said they could not see his face again if they did not bring Benjamin with them.

Jacob was sad when he heard all these things. He said that Joseph was dead and another boy was in prison. Now they wanted to take Benjamin away from him. He said he would not let Benjamin go. He said if anything happened to Benjamin he would cry until he died.

QUESTIONS

1. How did Joseph treat his brothers?
2. Why did he say they had come?
3. What did the brothers say to him?
4. How long did Joseph keep them in prison?
5. Why did he keep one of them when he sent the others home?
6. What did Joseph give to them?
7. On the way home what did they find in their sacks?
8. Why were they afraid?
9. What did they tell Jacob when they got home?
10. Why did they say they would have to take Benjamin next time?
11. What did Jacob say?
12. How long did Jacob say he would cry if anything happened to Benjamin?

Benjamin Goes to Egypt
(Gen. 43:1-34)

Jacob and his family used up all the food that they had bought in the land of Egypt. Jacob called his boys and told them to go back and buy more food. They said they would go if he would let them take Benjamin with them. The ruler had said that they could not see his face again if their youngest brother was not with them.

Jacob did not want Benjamin to go. He was afraid something would happen to him. One of his boys, whose name was Judah, said, "Let me take Benjamin and I will look after him. I will not let anything happen to him." Jacob thought Judah would take care of him, so he said that Benjamin could go.

Jacob told them to take a present to the ruler of Egypt. Perhaps he would treat them better. He told them to take two times as much money for the food. Then they could pay back what they had found in their sacks.

The brothers went on their way and came to Egypt. They stood before Joseph. They did not know that he was Joseph, but he knew them.

Joseph told his servants to fix a big dinner. He said that the men were going to eat with him. The brothers were very afraid when they heard that they were to eat with the ruler. They came to the door of Joseph's house. They saw a servant and told him about the money that they had found in their sacks. They told him that they had brought it back with them. The servant said, "Do not be afraid. God gave you back your money."

The ruler sent and brought the

brother out of prison. He had them all sit down at the table to eat. They were all surprised when they sat down. They were seated according to their ages, beginning at the oldest and going on down to the youngest. They did not know how the ruler could know how old they were.

Joseph asked them if their father were still living. He said, "Is he well?" They said, "He is well." He saw Benjamin and said, "Is this your youngest brother?" He was so happy when he saw his youngest brother that he wanted to cry. He turned and went into another room and cried. He washed his face and came back into the room.

He gave all his brothers plenty of food to eat. He gave Benjamin five times as much as the others because he loved him best of all.

QUESTIONS

1. Why did Jacob tell his boys to go back to Egypt?
2. Who did they say must go with them?
3. Why did Jacob not want Benjamin to go?
4. What did Judah say?
5. What did Jacob say for them to take to the ruler?
6. What did Joseph tell his servants to do?
7. Why were his brothers afraid?
8. What did they say to the servant?
9. Who did the servant say gave them back their money?
10. Whom did Joseph ask about?
11. What did he do when he saw Benjamin?
12. How much did he give Benjamin to eat?

The Silver Cup
(Gen. 44:1 - 45:3)

The next morning the brothers started back to their home in Canaan. Joseph told his servant to put their money back in their sacks again. He told the servant to put his silver cup in Benjamin's sack.

When the brothers had been gone for a little while, Joseph sent his servant after them. The servant went very fast and soon caught up with them. He asked them why they had stolen his master's silver cup. The brothers said they had not stolen the cup. They did not know anything about it. The servant wanted to look in their sacks. They did not care because they did not think they had the cup. They said if the servant found the cup he could kill the one who had it. The rest of them would

become servants. The servant said he would keep just the one who had the cup and the rest could go home.

The men all opened their sacks for the servant to see. He looked in all their sacks, beginning with the oldest and going on to the youngest. He found it in Benjamin's sack.

The brothers were very surprised and very sad. They did not understand what had happened. They tore their clothes. They got on their donkeys and went back to the city. They came to Joseph's house. Joseph was there waiting for them. He hoped they would come back. They fell down before him on the ground. He spoke roughly to them and said, "Why have you done this? Did you not know that I would find it out?"

One of the boys, whose name was Judah, said, "God has found out all the bad things we have done. Now we will be your servants." Joseph said, "No, I will keep the one who had the cup. All the rest of you may go back to your home."

Judah came near to him and said, "I promised my father before I left home that I would take care of Benjamin. I promised him that I would not let anything happen to him. If I go back home without him, my father will be so sad that he will die. Let Benjamin go back and let me stay. I will be a servant in his place. I cannot look at my father if the boy is not with me."

Joseph was very happy when he heard what Judah said. He knew now that the brothers were not wicked. He knew that they did not hate Benjamin as they once hated Joseph.

He told his servants to leave the

room. He cried with a loud voice and said, "I am Joseph." The brothers were so surprised that they could not say a word. They were afraid.

QUESTIONS

1. What did Joseph tell his servant to do?
2. What did he say for him to put in Benjamin's sack?
3. When the brothers had been gone a little while, what did Joseph do?
4. What did the servant say to them?
5. What did the brothers say they would do if the servant found the cup?
6. Where did the servant find the cup?
7. What did the brothers do?
8. Who was waiting for them when they came back?
9. What did Joseph say he would do with the one who had the cup?
10. What did Judah say?
11. What did Joseph say to them in a loud voice?
12. How did the brothers feel?

Joseph Sends for Jacob
(Gen. 45:3-24)

Joseph cried out in a very loud voice. All his servants and all the people in the king's house heard him. He said to his brothers, "I am Joseph." They were so surprised and so afraid that they could not talk to him. He said, "I am Joseph, your brother, whom you sold. Is my father still living?" The brothers could not say a word. Joseph said, "Come near to me." They could not believe what they heard. They could not believe that their brother Joseph was ruler over all the land of Egypt. At last they came near to him, and he hugged and kissed all of them. He talked to them in the language that they could understand. He told them not to be angry with themselves. He said that God had been with him and had sent him into Egypt to save their lives.

He told them that there would be five more years of famine when nothing would grow in the fields. God had sent Joseph into Egypt to save food to feed his own family.

Joseph told his brothers to hurry back home and tell his father that he was alive and that he was ruler over all the land of Egypt. He told them to bring his father and all that they had and come down into Egypt. Then they could live till the famine was over and Joseph would take care of them.

The brothers were very afraid. Joseph said, "Do not be afraid. You meant to do wrong to me, but God made everything turn out to be good." He kissed all of them and he had to cry when he kissed Benjamin. He loved Benjamin best of all, and the other brothers were glad.

The brothers talked a long time to Joseph. They were not afraid any more. They knew that Joseph was not angry with them.

Pharaoh heard that Joseph's brothers had come. He was very glad. He told Joseph to tell his brothers to go back to their home and get their father and their wives and their little children. He said for them to bring everything they had down into Egypt. He said they could have the very best part of the land to live in. They could have the best food for themselves and their sheep and cows. He gave them wagons to take back with them so they could bring everything down to Egypt.

Joseph gave his brothers plenty of food for the trip home. He gave the wagons of Pharaoh to them to take. He gave each one of the brothers a new suit of clothes. He gave Benjamin five suits of clothes and three hundred pieces of money. He told them to be careful on the way home so nothing would happen to them.

QUESTIONS

1. Who heard Joseph crying?
2. What did Joseph tell his brothers?
3. Why did he tell them not to be sad?
4. Why did he say God had sent him to Egypt?
5. Why did he tell them to hurry home?
6. What did Joseph do to show he was happy?
7. How did he say that God had made everything turn out?
8. How did Pharaoh feel when he heard that Joseph's brothers had come?
9. What did he say for Joseph to tell his brothers?
10. What part of the land did he say they could have?
11. What did Joseph give them for the trip?
12. What did he give to Benjamin?

Jacob Goes to Egypt
(Gen. 45:25 - 46:34)

The brothers came back to their home in the land of Canaan. They told their father Jacob all that had happened to them. They told him that Joseph was still alive and that he was ruler over all the land of Egypt. Jacob could not believe what they said. He was so surprised that he fainted. He thought Joseph was dead. He thought a wild animal had killed him. He could not believe that Joseph was ruler over all Egypt.

Jacob saw the wagons that Pharaoh had sent and all the food. Then he believed what his sons said. He said, "My son Joseph is still alive. I will go and see him again before I die."

Jacob took all his family and all his sheep and all his cows and started on

his way to Egypt. On the way he
stopped at a place called Beersheba.
There he built an altar and offered a
sacrifice to God. He spent the night
there.

In the night God came to him and
said, "I am the God of your father. Do
not be afraid to go down into Egypt. I
will make of you a great nation. I will
go down with you into Egypt. I will
also surely bring you up out of the land
again. Joseph will put his hands on
your eyes."

Jacob knew then that it was good for

him to go to Egypt because God was going to be with him. He got up the next morning and took all his things and went on down into Egypt.

Jacob had lots of children. His children were grown up and they had lots of children. There was a crowd of people who went into Egypt. Joseph and his wife and his two sons were already in Egypt, so Jacob had seventy people in his family.

Joseph heard that his father and all

his family were coming. He got in his chariot and hurried to meet them. He was in a hurry to see his father because he had not seen him for a long, long time. When he saw him, he ran to him and hugged his neck. He was so happy that he cried for a long time. Jacob cried, too. He was happy because Joseph was alive and that he could see him again. He said, "Now I am ready to die because I have seen your face again. Now I know that you are still alive."

QUESTIONS

1. What did the brothers tell Jacob?
2. What did Jacob do?
3. Why was Jacob so surprised?
4. What did he say when he saw the wagons and food?
5. Where did Jacob stop on the way?
6. What did he do there?
7. Who spoke to him?
8. What did God tell him?
9. How many people were there in Jacob's family?
10. What did Joseph do when he heard that Jacob was coming?
11. What did Jacob and Joseph do when they met?
12. What did Jacob say?

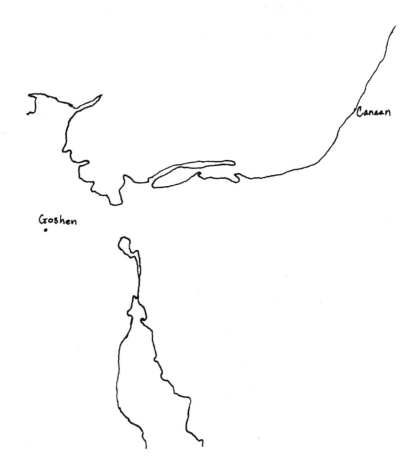

Canaan

Goshen

Jacob Sees Pharaoh
(Gen. 47:1-12)

Part of the land of Egypt was called the land of Goshen. It was the very best part of the land. There was plenty of good grass and fresh water there for sheep and cows and goats. Jacob and his boys were shepherds. That means that they had lots of sheep and cows and goats and took care of them. They needed plenty of grass and water. If they lived in the land of Egypt they could not move around from place to place as they had done in the land of Canaan. There were too many people living in Egypt. There would not be room for everybody to move around. They would have to stay in the same place all the time. They needed a very good place where there would always be plenty of grass and water.

247

King Pharaoh heard that Joseph's family was coming. He said they could have the very best part of the land because he loved Joseph so much.

Joseph took his father Jacob and five of his brothers to see the king. Pharaoh asked them what kind of work they did. They told him that they were shepherds. He told them that they could live in the land of Goshen because that was the best part of the land for shepherds. Pharaoh asked Jacob how old he was. Jacob said, "I am not very old. I have not lived as long as my father did. I am only one hundred thirty years old." That sounds like a very old age to us, but in those days people lived much longer than they do now.

Joseph took his father and his brothers and all that they had and put them in the land of Goshen. He gave them plenty of food and all the things they needed. He took care of them all the time that the famine lasted.

QUESTIONS

1. What kind of work did Jacob and his boys do?
2. What was the best part of the land of Egypt?
3. Why did Jacob need to live in the land of Goshen?
4. Why could they not move around in the land of Egypt?
5. What part of the land did Pharaoh say they could have?
6. How many of his brothers did Joseph take to Pharaoh?
7. What did Pharaoh ask them?
8. What did Pharaoh say to Jacob?
9. How old was Jacob?
10. Who did Jacob say had lived longer than he?
11. What did Joseph give to his father and his brothers?
12. How long did he take care of them?

The Famine Continues
(Gen. 47:13-26)

The famine lasted for seven years just as Joseph said it would. At first the people used up the food they had in their houses. Then they came to Joseph to buy food. You remember that Joseph had stored up all the extra food in store houses. He had stored up so much that they could not count it. The people brought money to buy food until after a while their money was all gone.

When their money was all gone, the people came to Joseph and said, "Our money is all gone. We do not have any to buy food. We shall die if we do not have food." Joseph said, "Bring your

sheep, your cows, your horses, and all your animals and give them to the king. Then I will give you food."

They brought all their animals, and Joseph gave them food. After a while all the cows and all the sheep and all the horses belonged to Pharaoh.

Soon the people had sold all their animals to Pharaoh. They had none left with which to buy food. They came to Joseph again and said, "All our money is gone. All our cows and sheep are gone. We have nothing left now but our bodies and our land, but we must have food to eat."

Joseph said he would take their land and give them food for their land. He bought all their land for the king. Soon all the land of Egypt belonged to the king. The people said, "We will be your servants if you will just give us food to eat."

The king took all the people and put them in the cities. Then he could feed them and take care of them so that they would not die. The people said that Joseph had saved their lives and they loved him.

Joseph gave all the people seed to plant in their fields so that things could grow again after the famine was over. He said they could use the land just as though it belonged to them. Each year they were to give part of everything they raised to Pharaoh because the land was his. They were to give part to him and keep the rest for themselves and for their children.

QUESTIONS

1. How long did the famine last?
2. Who had stored up all the food?
3. What did the people bring with which to buy food?
4. What did the people say when their money was all gone?
5. What did Joseph tell them to bring?
6. After a while who owned all the animals?
7. After the animals were gone, what did Joseph say they could use to buy food?
8. Soon all the land belonged to whom?
9. What did the people say they would do?
10. Where did the king put the people?
11. What did the people say that Joseph had done?
12. When the famine was over, what were the people to give to Pharaoh each year?

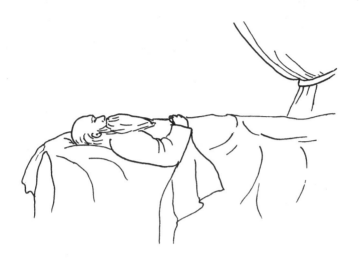

The Death of Jacob
(Gen. 48:1 - 50:3)

Jacob lived in the land of Egypt for seventeen years. It was a good land. Jacob and his family became rich with many cows and sheep and other things. More little children were born to Jacob's children so that there were many people in the land.

After a while the time came for Jacob to die. He was an old man. He called Joseph and said, "I am going to die. I want you to promise me something before I die." He wanted Joseph to promise that he would not bury him in Egypt. He wanted to go back to his old home in the land of Canaan. He wanted to be buried in the place where they had buried his wife Leah, his father Isaac, his mother Rebekah, his grandfather Abraham, and his grandmother Sarah. That would be a good place to be buried. Joseph said, "I will do just what you have said."

Jacob called all his boys to him and blessed them. He called Joseph's two boys to him and blessed them. He said they were his boys, too, and he would count them just the same as his own boys. He told them that God would be with them and would some day take them all out of the land of Egypt. He said God would take them back to the

land of Canaan and give them all the land to be their own.

Jacob finished blessing his sons. He made them promise again that they would take him back to his old home to bury him. He then laid down on his bed and died.

Joseph fell down by the bed and cried. All his brothers cried, too. The king and all his people heard that Jacob was dead. They cried because they were sorry for Joseph. They cried a long, long time.

Joseph told Pharaoh that his father had made him promise to take him back to his old home to bury him. He asked Pharaoh if he might go. Pharaoh told him that he could go. So Joseph and all his brothers and the servants of Pharaoh and a great crowd of Pharaoh's people went up to the land of Canaan to bury Jacob. They took him to the very place where he wanted to go. There they buried him just as they had promised. When they had buried him, they went back to the land of Egypt.

QUESTIONS

1. How long did Jacob live in the land of Egypt?
2. What did they get because the land was good?
3. What happened when Jacob was old?
4. What did he want Joseph to promise?
5. With whom did he want to be buried?
6. What did he do when he called his boys?
7. What did he say about Joseph's boys?
8. What did he say God would do?
9. What did he make them promise again?
10. What did Joseph and all his brothers do when Jacob died?
11. Who went with them to bury Jacob?
12. Where did they bury him?

The End of the Story
(Gen. 50:4-26)

When Jacob was dead, Joseph's brothers began to be worried about something. They had done something very, very wrong a long time ago. Now they were worried about it. Do you remember that they had sold Joseph when they were all young? Now they were all grown up men and some of them were getting old. They said they were afraid now since their father was dead that Joseph would hate them. They were afraid he would want to do something bad to them because they had treated him bad a long time ago.

They went to Joseph and told him that they were sorry that they had done wrong. They wanted him to keep on being good to them and not to treat them bad. They said their father did not want

Joseph to hate them and do bad things to them.

Joseph was very sad when they said those things to him. He was not angry with them. He loved them and he was not going to be bad to them. He cried, and when he cried, his brothers went and bowed down before him. They said, "We are your servants." Joseph said, "Do not be afraid." He said they had meant to do evil to him but God had turned it into good. God had helped

him save their lives by taking care of them when the famine came. He talked very kindly to them so that they were not afraid any more.

The time came for Joseph to die. He called his brothers to come to him and he talked to them. He told them that God would be with them and would sometime take them back to the land of Canaan. He said that God would give them the land of Canaan to be their very own. He made them promise that they would take his body with them when God took them out of the land of Egypt. He wanted to be buried in the land of Canaan but he did not want to be taken back until all his people could go, too.

Joseph died when he was a hundred years old. They fixed him ready to bury and put him in a coffin down in Egypt.

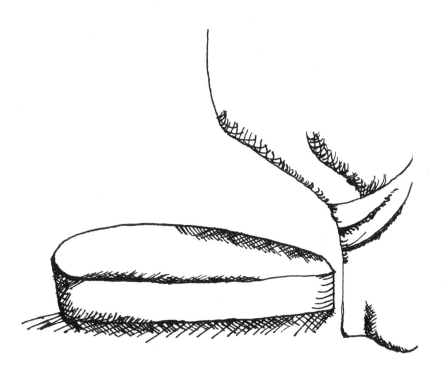

QUESTIONS

1. When Jacob was dead, how did the brothers feel?
2. What had they done that was very, very bad?
3. Why were the brothers afraid?
4. What did they say to Joseph?
5. How did Joseph feel when he heard those things?
6. What did the brothers do when Joseph cried?
7. What did they say?
8. What did Joseph say they meant to do?
9. How did God change it?
10. How had Joseph saved their lives?
11. When Joseph was ready to die, what did he do?
12. What did he say God would do to them?
13. What did he tell them to do when they were ready to leave Egypt?
14. How old was Joseph when he died?

CPSIA information can be obtained
at www.ICGtesting.com
Printed in the USA
JSHW040904150821
17716JS00002B/127